THE
DISCOVERY, SETTLEMENT

And prefent State of

KENTUCKE:

AND

An ESSAY towards the TOPOGRAPHY, and NATURAL HISTORY of that important Country:

To which is added,

An APPENDIX,

CONTAINING,

I. The ADVENTURES of Col. *Daniel Boon,* one of the firſt Settlers, comprehending every important Occurrence in the political Hiſtory of that Province.

II The MINUTES of the *Piankaſhaw* council, held at *Poſt St. Vincents, April* 15, 1784.

III. An ACCOUNT of the *Indian* Nations inhabiting within the Limits of the Thirteen United States, their Manners and Cuſtoms, and Reflections on their Origin.

IV. The STAGES and DISTANCES between *Philadelphia* and the Falls of the *Ohio;* from *Pittſburg* to *Penſacola* and ſeveral other Places. —The Whole illuſtrated by a new and accurate MAP of *Kentucke* and the Country adjoining, drawn from actual Surveys.

By *JOHN FILSON.*

Wilmington, Printed by JAMES ADAMS, 1784.

Printing Statement:

Due to the very old age and scarcity of this book, many of the pages may be hard to read due to the blurring of the original text, possible missing pages, missing text and other issues beyond our control.

Because this is such an important and rare work, we believe it is best to reproduce this book regardless of its original condition.

Thank you for your understanding.

WE the Subscribers, inhabitants of Kentucke, and well acquainted with the country from its first settlement, at the request of the author of this book, and map, have carefully revised them, and recommend them to the public, as exceeding good performances, containing as accurate a description of our country as we think can possibly be given; much preferable to any in our knowledge extant; and think it will be of great utility to the publick. Witness our hands this 12th day of May, Anno Domini 1784,

DANIEL BOON,

LEVI TODD,

JAMES HARROD.

PREFACE.

THE generality of those geographers, who have attempted a map, or description of America, seem either to have had no knowledge of Kentucke, or to have neglected it, although a place of infinite importance: And the rest have proceeded so erroneously, that they have left the world as much in darkness as before. Many are the mistakes, respecting the subject of this work, in all other maps which I have yet seen; whereas I can truly say, I know of none in that which I here present to the world either from my own particular knowledge, or from the information of those gentlemen with whose assistance I have been favoured, and who have been well acquainted with the country since the first settlement. When I visited Kentucke, I found it so far to exceed my expectations, although great, that I concluded it was a pity, that the world had not adequate information of it. I conceived that a proper description, and map of it, were objects highly interesting to the United States; and therefore, incredible as it may appear to some, I must declare, that this performance is not published from lucrative motives, but solely to inform the world of the happy climate, and

plentiful

plentiful soil of this favoured region. And I ima-
gine the reader will believe me the more easily when I
inform him, that I am not an inhabitant of Kentuc-
ke, but having been there some time, by my acquain-
tance in it, am sufficiently able to publish the truth,
and from principle, have cautiously endeavoured to
avoid every species of falsehood. The consciousness of
this encourages me to hope for the public candour,
where errors may possibly be found. The three
gentlemen honouring this work with their recommen-
dation, Col. Boon, Col. Todd, and Col. Harrod, were
among the first settlers, and perfectly well acquaint-
ed with the country. To them I acknowledge myself
much indebted for their friendly assistance in this work,
which they chearfully contributed with a disinterested
view of being serviceable to the public. My thanks
are more especially due to Col. Boon, who was earli-
er acquainted with the subject of this performance
than any other now living, as appears by the ac-
count of his adventures, which I esteemed curious
and interesting, and therefore have published them
from his own mouth. Much advantage may possi-
bly arise to the possessor of this book, as those who
wish to travel in Kentucke will undoubtedly find it
a Compleat Guide. To such I affirm, that there is
nothing mentioned or described but what they will
find true. Conscious that it would be of general utility,
I have omitted nothing, and been exceeding particu-
lar in every part. That it may have the desired
effect, is the sincere wish of

JOHN FILSON.

THE

DISCOVERY, PURCHASE

AND

SETTLEMENT,

OF

KENTUCKE.

THE firſt white man we have certain accounts of, who diſcovered this province, was one James M'Bride, who, in company with ſome others, in the year 1754, paſſing down the Ohio in Canoes, landed at the mouth of Kentucke river, and there marked a tree, with the firſt letters of his name, and the date, which remain to this day. Theſe men reconnoitred the country, and returned home with the pleaſing news of their diſcovery of the beſt tract of land in North-America, and probably in the world.

world. From this period it remained concealed till about the year 1767, when one John Finley, and some others, trading with the Indians, fortunately travelled over the fertile region, now called Kentucke, then but known to the Indians, by the name of the Dark and Bloody Ground, and sometimes the Middle Ground. This country greatly engaged Mr. Finley's attention. Some time after, disputes arising between the Indians and traders, he was obliged to decamp; and returned to his place of residence in North-Carolina, where he communicated his discovery to Col. Daniel Boon, and a few more, who conceiving it to be an interesting object, agreed in the year 1769 to undertake a journey in order to explore it. After a long fatiguing march, over a mountainous wilderness, in a westward direction, they at length arrived upon its borders; and from the top of an eminence, with joy and wonder, descried the beautiful landscape of Kentucke. Here they encamped, and some went to hunt provisions, which were readily procured, there being plenty of game, while Col. Boon and John Finley made a tour through the country, which they found far exceeding their expectations, and returning to camp, informed their companions of their discoveries: But in spite of this promising beginning, this company, meeting with nothing but hardships and adver-

sity,

fity, grew exceedingly difheartened, and was plundered, difperfed, and killed by the Indians, except Col. Boon, who continued an inhabitant of the wildernefs until the year 1771, when he returned home.

About this time Kentucke had drawn the attention of feveral gentlemen. Doctor Walker of Virginia, with a number more, made a tour weftward for difcoveries, endeavouring to find the Ohio river ; and afterwards he and General Lewis, at Fort Stanwix, purchafed from the Five Nations of Indians the lands lying on the north fide of Kentucke. Col. Donaldfon, of Virginia, being employed by the State to run a line from fix miles above the Long Ifland, on Holftein, to the mouth of the great Kenhawa, and finding thereby that an extenfive tract of excellent country would be cut off to the Indians, was folicited, by the inhabitants of Clench and Holftein, to purchafe the lands lying on the north fide of Kentucke river from the Five Nations. This purchafe he compleated for five hundred pounds, fpecie. It was then agreed, to fix a boundary line, running from the long Ifland on Holftein to the head of Kentucke river: thence down the fame to the mouth ; thence up the Ohio, to the mouth of Great Kenhawa ; but this valuable purchafe the State refufed to confirm.

B

Col.

Col. Henderſon, of North-Carolina, being informed of this country by Col. Booil, he, and ſome other gentlemen, held a treaty with the Cherokee Indians at Wataga, in March 1775, and then purchaſed from them the lands lying on the ſouth ſide of Kentucke river for goods, at valuable rates, to the amount of ſix thouſand pounds, ſpecie.

Soon after this purchaſe, the State of Virginia took the alarm, agreed to pay the money Col. Donaldſon had contracted for, and then diſputed Col. Henderſon's right of purchaſe, as a private gentlemen of another ſtate, in behalf of himſelf : However, for his eminent ſervices to this country, and for having been inſtrumental in making ſo valuable an acquiſition to Virginia, thar ſtate was pleaſed to reward him with a tract of land, at the mouth of Green River, to the amount of two hundred thouſand acres ; and the ſtate of North-Carolina gave him the like quantity in Powel's Valley. This region was formerly claimed by various tribes of Indians ; whoſe title, if they had any, originated in ſuch a manner, as to render it doubtful which ought to poſſeſs it : Hence this fertile ſpot became an object of contention, a theatre of war, from which it was properly denominated the Bloody-Grounds. Their contentions not being likely to decide the Right to any particular tribe, as
ſoon

foon as Mr. Henderfon and his friends propofed to purchafe, the Indians agreed to fell; and notwithftanding the valuable Confideration they received, have continued ever fince troublefome neighbours to the new fettlers.

SITUATION and BOUNDARIES.

KENTUCKE is fituated, in its central part, near the latitude of 38 °½ north, and 85° weft longitude, and lying within the fifth climate, its longeft day is 14 hours 40 minutes. It is bounded on the north by great Sandy-creek; by the Ohio on the N. W. by North-Carolina on the fouth; and by the Cumberland mountain on the eaft, being upwards of 250 miles in length, and two hundred in breadth; and is at prefent divided into three counties, Lincoln, Fayette and Jefferfon; of which Fayette and Jefferfon are bounded by the Ohio, and the river Kentucke feparates Fayette on its north fide from the other two. There are at prefent eight towns laid off, and building; and more are propofed.

Louifville, at the Falls of Ohio, and Beardstown, are in Jefferfon county; Harrodfburg, Danville, and Boons-burrow, in Lincoln county; Lexington, Lees-town, and Greenville, in Fayette county; the two laft being on Kentucke river. At thefe and many other places, on

this

this and other rivers, infpecting-houfes are eftablifhed for Tobacco, which may be cultivated to great advantage; although not altogether the ftaple commodity of the country.

R I V E R S.

THE beautiful river Ohio, bounds Kentucke in its whole length, being a mile and fometimes lefs in breadth, and is fufficient to carry boats of great burthen. Its general courfe is fouth 60 degrees weft; and in its courfe it receives numbers of large and fmall rivers, which pay tribute to its glory. The only difadvantage this fine river has, is a rapid, one mile and an half long, and one mile and a quarter broad, called the Falls of Ohio. In this place the river runs over a rocky bottom, and the defcent is fo gradual, that the fall does not probably in the whole exceed twenty feet. In fome places we may obferve it to fall a few feet. When the ftream is low, empty boats only can pafs and repafs this rapid; their lading muft be tranfported by land; but when high, boats of any burthen may pafs in fafety. Excepting this place, there is not a finer river in the world for navigation by boats. Befides this, Kentucke is watered by eight fmaller rivers, and many large and fmall creeks, as may be eafily feen in the map.

Licking

Licking River heading in the mountains with Cumberland River, and the North Branch of Kentucke, runs in a N. W. direction for upwards of a hundred miles, collecting its filver ftreams from many branches, and is about one hundred yards broad at its mouth.

Red River heads and interlocks with the main branch of Licking, and flows in a S. Weft courfe into Kentucke River, being about fixty miles long, and fixty yards wide at its mouth.

The Kentucke River rifes with three heads from a mountainous part of the Country. Its northern branch interlocks with Cumberland; runs half way in a weftern direction, and the other half N. wefterly. It is amazingly crooked, upwards of two hundred miles in length, and about one hundred and fifty yards broad.

Elkhorn is a fmall river which empties itfelf into Kentucke in a N. W. by W. courfe; is about fifty miles long, and fifty yards broad at the mouth.

Dick's River joins the Kentucke in a N. Weft direction; is about forty-five miles long, and forty-five yards wide at its mouth. This river curioufly heads and interlocks its branches with Salt River, Green River, and the waters
of

of Rock-caſtle River.—Salt River riſes at four different places near each other. The windings of this river are curious, rolling its ſtreams round a ſpacious tract of fine land, and uniting almoſt fifteen miles before they approach the Ohio, and twenty miles below the Falls. It is amazingly crooked, runs a weſtern courſe near ninety miles, and is about eighty yards wide at the mouth.

Green River interlocking with the heads of Dick's River, as mentioned above, is alſo a-mazingly crooked, keeps a weſtern courſe for upwards of one hundred and fifty miles, and is about eighty yards wide at its mouth, which is about two hundred and twenty miles below the Falls.

Cumberland River, interlocks with the north-ern branch of Kentucke, as aforeſaid, and rol-ling round the other arms of Kentucke, among the mountains, in a ſouthern courſe for one hundred miles; then in a ſouth weſtern courſe for above one hundred miles; then in a ſouth-ern and S. weſtern courſe for about two hun-dred and fifty more, finds the Ohio, four hun-dred and thirteen miles below the Falls. At the ſettlements it is two hundred yards broad; and at its mouth three hundred, having paſ-
fed

fed through North-Carolina in about half its
courfe.

The Great Kenhawa, or New River, rifes in
North-Carolina, runs a northern, and N. Weft
courfe for upwards of four hundred miles, and
finds the Ohio four hundred miles above the
Falls. It is about five hundred yards wide at
its mouth. Thefe two rivers are juft mentioned,
being beyond our limits. They run contrary
courfes, are exceeding large, and it is worth
notice, that Clench, Holftein, Nolachuckey, and
French-Broad rivers, take their rife between
thefe two, or rather weftward of New River,
fome of them rifing and interlocking with it;
and when they meet, form what is called the
Tenefe, or Cherokee River, which runs a weftern courfe, and finds the Ohio twelve miles
below Cumberland River. It is very large, and
has fpacious tracts of fine land.

These rivers are navigable for boats almoft
to their fources, without rapids, for the greateft part of the year. This country is generally level, and abounding with limeftone,
which ufually lies about fix feet deep, except in
hollows, where ftreams run, where we find the
rock in the bottom of the channel.

The fprings and ftreams leffen in June, and
continue

continue low, hindering navigation, until November, when the autumnal rains soon prepare the rivers for boats, and replenish the whole country with water; but although the streams decrease, yet there is always sufficient for domestic uses. There are many fine springs, that never fail; every farmer has a good one at least; and excellent wells may easily be dug.

Nature of the SOIL.

THE country, in some parts, is nearly level; in others not so much so; in others again hilly, but moderately, and in such places there is most water. The levels are not like a carpet, but interspersed with small risings, and declivities, which form a beautiful prospect. A great part of the soil is amazingly fertile; some not so good, and some poor. The inhabitants distinguish its quality by first, second, and third rate lands; and scarcely any such thing as a marsh or swamp is to be found. There is a ridge, where Kentucke rises, nearly of the size of a mountain, which in the map we have represented as such.

All the land below the Great Kenhawa until we come near the waters of Licking River is broken, hilly, and generally poor; except in some valleys, and on Little and Big Sandy
creeks

creeks, where there is fome firft rate land, but moftly fecond and third rate. It is faid, that near this water is found a pure falt rock. Upon the north branch of Licking, we find a great body of firft rate land. This ftream runs nearly parallel to the Ohio for a confiderable diftance, and is about feven miles from the mouth of Limeftone Creek, where is a fine harbour for boats coming down the Ohio, and now a common landing. It is fixty-five miles from Lexington, to which there is a large waggon road. The main branch of Licking, is about twenty-two miles from Limeftone. On this ftream we find fome firft, but moftly fecond and third rate lands, and towards its head fomething hilly. There we find the Blue Licks, two fine falt fprings, where great plenty of falt may be made. Round thefe licks, the foil is poor for fome diftance, being much impregnated with falt.

The fouthern branch of Licking, and all its other arms, as appears in the map, fpread through a great body of firft, and fome fecond rate land, where there is abundance of cane, and fome falt licks, and fprings. On thefe feveral branches of Licking, are good mill-feats, and navigation to the Ohio, from the fork down to its mouth. The land is hilly, and generally

C   poor,

poor, yet along the ftreams and in valleys we find fome excellent land.

The Elkhorn lands are much efteemed, being fituated in a bend of Kentucke River, of great extent, in which this little river, or rather large creek, rifes. Here we find moftly firft rate land, and near the Kentucke River fecond and third rate. This great tract is beautifully fituated, covered with cane, wild rye, and clover; and many of the ftreams afford fine mill feats.

The lands below the mouth of Elkhorn, up Eagle Creek, and towards the Ohio, are hilly and poor, except thofe contained in a great bend of the Ohio, oppofite Great Miami, cut off, as appears in the map, by the Big-bone and Bank-lick creeks, interlocking, and running feparate courfes. Here we find a great deal of good land, but fomething hilly.

On Kentucke River we find many fertile valleys, or bottoms along the river, efpecially towards its rife. There is good land alfo on Red River, but towards the heads of this, and Kentucke, the foil is broken; but even here, we find in valleys, and along ftreams, a great deal of fruitful land. Generally the foil within a mile or two of Kentucke River is of the third

. and

and fourth rates; from about that diftance, as we leave it on either fide, we approach good lands. The country through which it winds its courfe, for the moft part, may be confidered as level to its banks, or rather precipices; from the brow of which, we behold the river, three and fometimes four hundred feet deep, like a great canal. For a more particular account of this, we refer the reader to where we treat of the curiofities of Kentucke.

Dick's River runs through a great body of firft rate land, abounding every where with cane, and affords many excellent mill feats. Many mills are already built on this ftream, fome of which are reprefented in the map, and will have a plentiful fupply of water in the dryeft feafons. The banks of this river, near its mouth, are fimilar to the banks of Kentucke. The feveral ftreams and branches of Salt River afford excellent mill feats. Thefe roll themfelves through a great tract of excellent land, but the country from the junction of thefe waters, and fome miles above towards the Ohio, which may be about twenty-five miles, is level and poor, and has abundance of ponds. For a confiderable diftance from the head of this river, the land is of the firft quality, well fituated, and abounds with fine cane. Upon this,

and

and Dick's River, the inhabitants are chiefly settled, it being the safest part of the country from
the incursions of the Indians.

Green River, affords excellent mill seats, and
a constant stream.   This is allowed to be the
best watered part of Kentucke. On its banks we
find many fine bottoms, some first rate, but
mostly second and third rate lands; and at some
distance, many knobs, ridges, and broken poor
land.   Below a creek, called Sinking Creek, on
this river, within fifty miles of Ohio, towards
Salt River, a great territory begins, called
Green River Barrens, extending to the Ohio.
Most of this is very good land, and level. It
has no timber, and little water, but affords
excellent pasturage for cattle. On some parts
of this river, we find abundance of cane, some
salt licks, and sulphureous and bituminous
springs. South of Green River, in the lands
reserved for the continental, and state troops of
Virginia, an exceeding valuable lead mine has
lately been discovered.   Iron ore is found on
Rough Creek, a stream running into this river.
That part of Cumberland River which is in the
Kentucke country, traverses a hilly poor land,
though in some parts we find good soil along its
sides. The other rivers I mentioned (viz. Great
Kenhawa, and Tenese) are not in the Kentucke
country, and therefore do not come properly
within my plan.   The

The reader, by cafting his eye upon the map, and viewing round the heads of Licking, from the Ohio, and round the heads of Kentucke, Dick's River, and down Green River to the Ohio, may view, in that great compafs of above one hundred miles fquare, the moft extraordinary country that the fun enlightens with his celeftial beams.

The Ohio River, the great refervoir of all the numerous rivers that flow into it from both fides, has many fine valleys along its fides ; and we obferve that oppofite to each of them there is a hill ; thefe hills and bottoms changing fides alternately. It only remains under this head to inform the reader, that there is a great body of firft rate land near the Falls, or Rapids, called Bare-grafs ; and it will be fufficient juft to mention that the country on the N. Weft fide of the Ohio, fome of the waters of which I have reprefented in the map, is allowed by all travellers to be a moft fertile, level country, and well watered.

AIR and CLIMATE.

THIS country is more temperate and healthy than the other fettled parts of America. In Summer it wants the fandy heats which Virginia and Carolina experience, and receives a fine air from

from its rivers. In Winter, which at most only lasts three months, commonly two, and is but seldom severe, the people are safe in bad houses; and the beasts have a good supply without fodder. The Winter begins about Christmas, and ends about the first of March, at farthest does not exceed the middle of that month. Snow seldom falls deep or lies long. The west winds often bring storms, and the east winds clear the sky; but there is no steady rule of weather in that respect as in the northern states. The west winds are sometimes cold and nitrous. The Ohio running in that direction, and there being mountains on that quarter, the westerly winds by sweeping along their tops, in the cold regions of the air, and over a long tract of frozen water, collect cold in their course, and convey it over the Kentucke country; but the weather is not so intensely severe as these winds bring with them in Pennsylvania. The air and seasons depend very much on the winds, as to heat and cold, dryness and moisture.

SOIL AND PRODUCE.

THE soil of Kentucke is of a loose, deep black mould, without sand, in the first rate lands about two or three feet deep, and exceeding luxurious in all its productions. In some places the mould inclines to brown. In some the wood, as

the

the natural confequence of too rich a foil, is of little value, appearing like dead timber and large ftumps in a field lately cleared. Thefe parts are not confiderable. The country in general may be confidered as well timbered, producing large trees of many kinds, and to be exceeded by no country in variety. Thofe which are peculiar to Kentucke are the fugar-tree, which grows in all parts in great plenty, and furnifhes every family with plenty of excellent fugar. The honey-locuft is curioufly furrounded with large thorny fpikes, bearing broad and long pods in form of peas, has a fweet tafte, and makes excellent beer.

The coffee-tree greatly refembles the black oak, grows large, and alfo bears a pod, in which is enclofed good coffee. The pappa-tree does not grow to a great fize, is a foft wood, bears a fine fruit much like a cucumber in fhape and fize, and taftes fweet. The cucumber-tree is fmall and foft, with remarkable leaves, bears a fruit much refembling that from which it is named. Black mulberry-trees are in abundance. The wild cherry-tree is here frequent, of a large fize, and fupplies the inhabitants with boards for all their buildings. Here alfo is the buck-eye, an exceeding foft wood, bearing a remarkable black fruit, and fome other kinds of trees not common elfewhere. Here is great plenty of fine cane, on which the cattle feed, and grow fat. This plant

in

in general grows from three to twelve feet high, of a hard substance, with joints at eight or ten inches distance along the stalk, from which proceed leaves resembling those of the willow. There are many cane brakes so thick and tall that it is difficult to pass through them. Where no cane grows there is abundance of wild-rye, clover, and buffalo-grass, covering vast tracts of country, and affording excellent food for cattle. The fields are covered with abundance of wild herbage not common to other countries. The Shawanese sallad, wild lettuce, and pepper-grass, and many more, as yet unknown to the inhabitants, but which, no doubt, have excellent virtues. Here are seen the finest crown-imperial in the world, the cardinal flower, so much extolled for its scarlet colour; and all the year, excepting the three Winter months, the plains and valleys are adorned with variety of flowers of the most admirable beauty. Here is also found the tulip-bearing laurel-tree, or magnolia, which has an exquisite smell, and continues to blossom and feed for several months together.

This country is richest on the higher lands, exceeding the finest low grounds in the settled parts of the continent. When cultivated it produces in common fifty and sixty bushels per acre; and I have heard it affirmed by credible persons, that above one hundred bushels of good corn

corn were produced from an acre in one feafon. The firft rate land is too rich for wheat till it has been reduced by four or five years cultivation.

Col. Harrod, a gentleman of veracity in Ken-tucke, has lately experienced the production of fmall grain, and affirms, that he had thirty-five bufhels of wheat, and fifty bufhels of rye per a-cre.

I think in common the land will produce a-bout thirty bufhels of wheat, and rye, upon a moderate computation, per acre; and this is the general opinion of the inhabitants. We may fuppofe that barley and oats will increafe abun-dantly; as yet they have not been fufficiently tried. The foil is very favourable to flax and hemp, turnips, potatoes and cotton, which grow in abundance; and the fecond, third and fourth rate lands, are as proper for fmall grain. Thefe accounts of fuch amazing fertility may, to fome, appear incredible, but are certainly true. Every hufbandman may have a good gar-den, or meadow, without water or manure, where he pleafes. The foil, which is not of a thir-fty nature, is commonly well fupplied with plen-tiful fhowers.

Iron ore and lead are found in abundance, but we do not hear of any filver or gold mine as yet dif-covered.   D   The

The weſtern waters produce plenty of fiſh and fowl. The fiſh common to the waters of the Ohio are the buffalo-fiſh, of a large ſize, and the cat-fiſh ſometimes exceeding one hundred weight. Salmons have been taken in Kentucke weighing thirty weight. The mullet, rock, perch, gar-fiſh, and eel, are here in plenty. It is ſaid that there are no trouts in the weſtern waters. Suckers, ſun-fiſh, and other hook-fiſh, are abundant ; but no ſhad, or herrings. We may ſuppoſe with a degree of certainty, that there are large ſubterraneous aqueducts ſtored with fiſh, from whence fine ſprings ariſe in many parts producing fine hook-fiſh in variety. On theſe waters, and eſpecially on the Ohio, the geeſe and ducks are amazingly numerous.

The land fowls are turkeys, which are very frequent, pheaſants, partridges, and ravens : The perraquet, a bird every way reſembling a parrot, but much ſmaller ; the ivory-bill wood-cock, of a whitiſh colour with a white plume, flies ſcreaming exceeding ſharp. It is aſſerted, that the bill of this bird is pure ivory, a circumſtance very ſingular in the plumy tribe. The great owl reſembles its ſpecies in other parts, but is remarkably different in its vociferation, ſometimes making a ſtrange, ſurpriſing noiſe, like a man in the moſt extreme danger and difficulty.

Serpents

Serpents are not numerous, and are such as are to be found in other parts of the continent, except the bull, the horned and the mockason snakes. Swamps are rare, and consequently frogs and other reptiles, common to such places. There are no swarms of bees, except such as have been introduced by the present inhabitants.

QUADRUPEDS.

AMONG the native animals are the urus, or zorax, described by Cesar, which we call a buffalo, much resembling a large bull, of a great size, with a large head, thick short crooked horns, and broader in his forepart than behind. Upon his shoulder is a large lump of flesh, covered with a thick bofs of long wool and curly hair, of a dark brown colour. They do not rise from the ground as our cattle, but spring up at once upon their feet; are of a broad make and clumsy appearance, with short legs, but run fast, and turn not aside for any thing when chafed, except a standing tree. They weigh from five to ten hundred weight, are excellent meat, supplying the inhabitants in many parts with beef, and their hides make good leather. I have heard a hunter assert, he saw above one thousand buffaloes at the Blue Licks at once; so numerous were they before the first settlers had wantonly sported away their lives. There still remains

mains a great number in the exterior parts of the fettlement. They feed upon cane and grafs, as other cattle, and are innocent harmlefs creatures.

There are ftill to be found many deer, elks and bears, within the fettlement, and many more on the borders of it. There are alfo panthers, wild-cats, and wolves.

The waters have plenty of beavers, otters, minks, and mufk-rats : Nor are the animals common to other parts wanting, fuch as foxes, rabbits, fquirrels, racoons, ground-hogs, pole-cats, and oppoffums. Moft of the fpecies of the domeftic quadrupeds have been introduced fince the fettlement, fuch as horfes, cows, fheep and hogs, which are prodigioufly multiplied, fuffered to run in the woods without a keeper, and only brought home when wanted.

INHABITANTS.

AN accurate account is kept of all the male inhabitants above the age of fixteen, who are rated towards the expences of the government by the name of Tithables ; from which, by allowing that thofe fo enrolled amount to a fourth part of the whole inhabitants, we may conclude that Kentucke contains, at prefent, upwards of thirty
thoufand

thoufand fouls : So amazingly rapid has been the fettlement in a few years. Numbers are daily arriving, and multitudes expected this Fall; which gives a well grounded expectation that the country will be exceedingly populous in a fhort time. The inhabitants, at prefent, have not extraordinary good houfes, as ufual in a newly fettled country.

They are, in general, polite, humane, hofpitable, and very complaifant. Being collected from different parts of the continent, they have a diverfity of manners, cuftoms and religions, which may in time perhaps be modified to one uniform. As yet united to the State of Virginia, they are governed by her wholefome laws, which are virtuoufly executed, and with excellent decorum. Schools for education are formed, and a college is appointed by act of Affembly of Virginia, to be founded under the conduct of truftees in Kentucke, and endowed with lands for its ufe. An excellent library is likewife beftowed upon this feminary, by the Rev. John Todd, of Virginia.

The Anabaptifts were the firft that promoted public worfhip in Kentucke; and the Prefbyterians have formed three large congregations near Harrod's ftation, and have engaged the Rev. David Rice, of Virginia, to be their paftor. At
Lexington

Lexington, 35 miles from thefe, they have form
ed another large congregation, and invited th
Rev. Mr. Rankin, of Virginia, to undertake tha
charge among them. At prefent there are no othe
religious focieties formed, although feveral othe
fects have numerous adherents. But from thef
early movements it is hoped that Kentucke wil
eminently fhine in learning and piety, which wil
fulfil the wifh of every virtuous citizen.

C U R I O S I T I E S.

A M O N G S T the natural curiofities of thi
country, the winding banks, or rather precipice
of Kentucke, and Dick's Rivers, deferve the firf
place. The aftonifhed eye there beholds almo
every where three or four hundred feet of a fo
lid perpendicular lime-ftone rock ; in fome part
a fine white marble, either curioufly arched, pil
lared or blocked up into fine building ftones
Thefe precipices, as was obferved before, are like
the fides of a deep trench, or canal ; the land a
bove being level, except where creeks fet in, anc
crowned with fine groves of red cedar. It is on
ly at particular places that this river can be crofi
ed, one of which is worthy of admiration ;
great road large enough for waggons made b
buffaloes, floping with an eafy defcent from th
top to the bottom of a very large fteep hill, a
or near the river above Lees-town.

Cave

Caves are found in this country amazingly large; in fome of which you may travel feveral miles under a fine limeftone rock, fupported by curious arches and pillars: In moft of them runs a ftream of water.

Near the head of Salt River a fubterranean lake or large pond has lately been difcovered. Col. Bowman fays, that he and a companion travelled in one four hours till he luckily came to the mouth again. The fame gentleman mentions another which operates like an air furnace, and contains much fulphur. An adventurer in any of thefe will have a perfect idea of primeval darknefs.

There appear to be great natural ftores of fulphur and falt in this country. A fpring at Boonfburrow conftantly emits fulphureous particles, and near the fame place is a falt fpring. There is another fulphureous fpring upon Four Mile Creek, a third upon Green River, and many others in different places, abounding with that ufeful mineral.

There are three fprings or ponds of bitumen near Green River, which do not form a ftream, but difgorge themfelves into a common refervoir, and when ufed in lamps anfwer all the purpofes of the fineft oil.

There

There are different places abounding with copperas, eafily procured, and in its prefent impure ftate fufficient for the ufe of the inhabitants; and when refined, equal to any in the world.

There is an allum bank on the fouth fide of Cumberland River, fituated at the bottom of a cliff of rocks projecting over it. In its prefent ftate it has the appearance and poffeffes the virtues of that mineral, and when purified is a beautiful allum.

Many fine falt fprings, whofe places appear in the map, conftantly emit water which, being manufactured, affords great quantities of fine falt. At prefent there is but one, called Bullet's Lick, improved, and this affords falt fufficient for all Kentucke, and exports fome to the Illinois. Salt fells at prefent for twenty fhillings per bufhel; but as fome other fprings are beginning to be worked, no doubt that neceffary article will foon be much cheaper. Drenne's-lick, the Big-bone, and the Blue-licks, fend forth ftreams of falt water. The Nob-lick, and many others, do not produce water, but confift of clay mixed with falt particles : To thefe the cattle repair, and reduce high hills rather to valleys than plains. The amazing herds of Buffaloes which refort thither, by their fize and number, fill the traveller with amazement and terror, efpecially when he

beholds

beholds the prodigious roads they have made from
all quarters, as if leading to fome populous city ;
the vaft fpace of land around thefe fprings defolat-
ed as if by a ravaging enemy, and hills reduced
to plains ; for the land near thofe fprings are
chiefly hilly. Thefe are truly curiofities, and the
eye can fcarcely be fatisfied with admiring them.

A medicinal fpring is found near the Big-bone
Lick, which has perfectly cured the itch by once
bathing ; and experience in time may difcover in
it other virtues. There is another of like nature
near Drenhen's-Lick.

Near Lexington are to be feen curious fepul-
chres, full of human fkeletons, which are thus fa-
bricated. Firft, on the ground are laid large
broad ftones ; on thefe were placed the bodies,
feparated from each other by broad ftones, covered
with others, which ferve as a bafis for the
next arrangement of bodies. In this order
they are built, without mortar, growing ftill nar-
rower to the height of a man. This method of
burying appears to be totally different from that
now practifed by the Indians. For our conjectures on this fubject we beg leave to refer to appendix No. 3.—At a falt fpring, near Ohio river,
very large bones are found, far furpaffing the
fize of any fpecies of animals now in America.
The head appears to have been about three

E   feet

feet long, the ribs seven, and the thigh bones a-
bout four ; one of which is repofited in the library in Philadelphia, and faid to weigh feventy-
eight pounds. The tufks are above a foot in
length, the grinders about five inches fquare,
and eight inches long. Thefe bones have equally
excited the amazement of the ignorant, and at-
tracted the attention of the philofopher. Speci-
mens of them have been fent both to France and
England, where they have been examined with the
greateft diligence, and found upon comparifon to
be remains of the fame fpecies of animals that
produced thofe other foffil bones which have been
difcovered in Tartary, Chili, and feveral other
places, both of the old and new continent.
What animal this is, and by what means its ruins are found in regions fo widely different, and
where none fuch exifts at prefent, is a queftion of
more difficult decifion. The ignorant and fuperftitious Tartars attribute them to a creature,
whom they call Maimon, who, they fay, ufually refides at the bottom of the rivers, and of
whom they relate many marvellous ftories ; but
as this is an affertion totally divefted of proof,
and even of probability, it has juftly been reject-
ed by the learned ; and on the other hand it is
certain, that no fuch amphibious quadruped exifts in our American waters. The bones themfelves bear a great refemblance to thofe of the e-
lephant. There is no other terreftrial animal now
known

known large enough to produce them. The tufks
with which they are equally furnifhed, equally
produce true ivory. Thefe external refemblances
have generally made fuperficial obfervers conclude, that they could belong to no other than
that prince of quadrupeds ; and when they firft
drew the attention of the world, philofophers
feem to have fubfcribed to the fame opinion.----
But if fo, whence is it that the whole fpecies has
difappeared from America? An animal fo laborious
and fo docile, that the induftry of the Peruvians,
which reduced to fervitude and fubjected to education fpecies fo vaftly inferior in thofe qualities,
as the Llama and the Paca, could never have over-
looked the elephant, if he had been to be found
in their country. Whence is it that thefe bones
are found in climates where the elephant, a native of the torrid zone, cannot even fubfift in his
wild ftate, and in a ftate of fervitude will not
propagate ? Thefe are difficulties fufficient to
ftagger credulity itfelf ; and at length produced
the enquiries of Dr. Hunter. That celebrated
anatomift, having procured fpecimens from the
Ohio, examined them with that accuracy for
which he is fo much diftinguifhed. He difcovered
a confiderable difference between the fhape and
ftructure of the bones, and thofe of the elephant.
He obferved from the form of the teeth, that
they muft have belonged to a carnivorous animal ;
whereas the habits of the elephant are foreign to
fuch

such sustenance, and his jaws totally unprovided with the teeth necessary for its use : And from the whole he concluded to the satisfaction of naturalists, that these bones belonged to a quadruped now unknown, and whose race is probably extinct, unless it may be be found in the extensive continent of New Holland, whose recesses have not yet been pervaded by the curiosity or avidity of civilized man. Can then so great a link have perished from the chain of nature? Happy we that it has. How formidable an enemy to the human species, an animal as large as the elephant, the tyrant of the forests, perhaps the devourer of man! Nations, such as the Indians, must have been in perpetual alarm. The animosities among the various tribes must have been suspended till the common enemy, who threatened the very existence of all, should be extirpated. To this circumstance we are probably indebted for a fact, which is perhaps singular in its kind, the extinction of a whole race of animals from the system of nature.

RIGHTS OF LAND.

THE proprietors of the Kentucke lands obtain their patents from Virginia, and their rights are of three kinds, viz. Those which arise from military service, from settlement and pre-emption, or from warrants from the treasury. The

military

military rights are held by officers, or their repre-
fentatives, as a reward for fervices done in one of
the two laft wars. The Settlement and pre-emption rights arife from occupation. Every man
who, before March, 1780, had remained in the
country one year, or raifed a crop of corn, was
allowed to have a fettlement of four hundred a-
cres, and a pre-emption adjoining it of one
thoufand acres. Every man who had only built
a cabbin, or made any improvement by himfelf or others, was entitled to a pre-emption
of one thoufand acres where fuch improvement
was made.

In March, 1780, the fettlement and pre-
emption rights ceafed, and treafury warrants, were afterwards iffued, authorizing their
poffeffor to locate the quantity of land mentioned in them, wherever it could be found
vacant in Virginia.

The mode of procedure in thefe affairs may be
inftructive to the reader. After the entry is made
in the land-office, there being one in each county, the perfon making the entry takes out a copy of the location, and proceeds to furvey when
he pleafes. The plot and certificate of fuch furvey muft be returned to the office within three
months after the furvey is made, there to be re-
corded; and a copy of the record muft be taken
out

out in twelve months, after the return of the furvey, and produced to the affiftant regifter of the land-office in Kentucke, where it muft lie fix months, that prior locators may have time and opportunity to enter a caveat, and prove their better right. If no caveat is entered in that time, the plot and certificate are fent to the land-office at Richmond, in Virginia, and three months more are allowed to have the patent returned to the owner.

The validity of the right of Virginia to this extenfive weftern territory has been difputed by fome, but without reafon. The weftern boundary of that ftate, by charter, reftricted by the treaty of Paris, in 1763, is fixed upon the Ohio River. She has purchafed the foil from the Indians, has firft fettled it, and eftablifhed wholefome laws for the regulation and government of the inhabitants; and therefore we conclude, that the right of Virginia to Kentucke is as permanent as the independence of America.

TRADE of KENTUCKE.

A CONVENIENT fituation for commerce is the grand hinge upon which the population, riches and happinefs of every country greatly depends. I believe many conceive the fituation of Kentucke to be unfavourable in this refpect. I confefs when I firft vifited this country I
was

was of the opinion of other misinformed men, that the beſt channel was from Philadelphia or Baltimore, by the way of Pittſburg,* and from thence down the Ohio ; and upon account of the difficulties and expences attending this route, for which there is no remedy, that goods would ever be dear. This opinion I have ſince reprobated, as the effeEt of ignorance of the trade up the Miſſiſſippi from New Orleans, or Mantchac, at the river or gut Iberville.

Thoſe who are acquainted with America know the Miſſiſſippi and Ohio rivers to be the key to the northern parts of the weſtern continent. Theſe are the principal channels through which that extenſive region, bathed by their waters, and enriched by the many ſtreams they receive, communicate with the ſea, and may truly be conſidered as the great paſſage made by the Hand of Nature for a variety of valuable purpoſes, and principally to promote the happineſs and benefit of mankind ; amongſt which, the conveyance of the produce of that immenſe and fertile country lying weſtward of the United States is not the leaſt. A ſhort deſcription of theſe rivers, and ſome others flowing into them, are objeEts ſubmitted to the reader's attention, in order to form

a

---

* From *Philadelphia to Pittſburg is a land-carriage of* 320 *miles, from Baltimore* 280.

a juft idea of the favourable commercial circumftances of that important country.

The Ohio river begins at Pittfburg, 320 miles
weft of Philadelphia, being there formed by the
junction of the Alleghany and Monangehela rivers,
and running a winding courfe of S. 60° Weft,
falls into the Miffiffippi 1074 miles, by the meanders of the river, below Pittfburg. The only obftruc-
tion to navigation on this river are the Rapids,
as defcribed before under the defcription of the
Kentucke rivers; but they are paffed in fafety
when the ftream is high.

The moft remarkable branches compofing the
head waters of Ohio are Red-ftone Creek, Cheat
River, and Yochiaghany. Thefe waters are navigable to a confiderable diftance above Pittfburg,
from November until June, and the Ohio a
month longer; but from great Kenhawa, which
is one hundred and ninety-fix miles and a half below Pittfburg, the ftream is navigable moft of the
year. Down this river great quantities of goods
are brought, and fome are conveyed up the Kentucke rivers, others on horfe-back or in waggons
to the fettled parts, and fold on an average at one
hundred pounds per cent. advance.

The current of the Ohio defcends about two
miles an hour in autumn, and when the waters
are

are high, about five miles. Thofe of the Kentucke rivers are much the fame, and without rapids, and are of immenfe value to the country,
affording fifh and fowl, and tranfportation of
the produce of the country to the beft market.
Thefe rivers increafe the Ohio more in depth.
than breadth. At its mouth it is not more than
one and a half mile in width, and enters the
Miffiffippi in a S. weft direction with a flow current, and a fine channel. This great river, at
the junction with the Ohio, runs in a S. eaft direction, and afterwards in a S. weft, having been a
little before joined by a greater river called Miffouri,* which runs in an eaftward direction
through Louifiana, and afterwards communicates
to the Miffiffippi‡ its own muddy and majef-
tic appearance. From the mouth of the Ohio to New
Orleans, a diftance not exceeding 460 miles in a
ftraight line, is about 856 by water. The depth
is, in common, eight or ten fathoms until you
approach its mouth, which empties itfelf by feveral channels into the gulf of Mexico. Here
the navigation is dangerous, on account of the
many iflands, fand-bars and logs, interfperfed in
its mouth, which is about twenty miles wide.

F   This

---

* *The Miffouri is fuppofed to be about* 3000 *miles*
long.

‡ *The Miffiffippi is faid to be about* 2500 *miles*
long.

This difadvantage may be remedied almoft in the fame manner that the ftream was difconcerted. The conflict between the fea and this mighty river, which brings down with its ftream great numbers of trees, mud, leaves, &c. caufes them to fubfide and form fhoals. One of thefe trees, ftopped by its roots or branches, will foon be joined by thoufands more, and fo fixed, that no human force is able to remove them. In time they are confolidated, every flood adds another layer to their height, forming iflands, which at length are covered with fhrubs, grafs and cane, and forcibly fhift the bed of the river. In this manner we fuppofe moft of the country on each fide of the Miffiffippi, below the Iberville, to have been formed, by iflands uniting to iflands, which in a fucceffion of time have greatly encroached on the fea, and produced an extenfive tract of country. If fome of the floating timber at the mouths of this river were moved into fome of the channels, numbers more would incorporate with them; and the current being impeded in thefe, the whole force of the river uniting, one important channel would forceably be opened, and fufficiently cleared, to admit of the moft excellent navigation.

About ninety-nine miles above Orleans is a fort, now called Mantchac by the Spaniards; formerly Fort Bute by the Englifh, who built it. Near this is
a large

a large gut, formed by the Miſſiſſippi, on the eaſt ſide, called Iberville ; ſome have dignified it with the name of River, when the Miſſiſſippi, its ſource, is high. This is navigable at moſt not above four months in the year for the firſt ten miles ; for three miles further it is from two to ſix feet in autumn, and from two to four fathoms the remaining part of the way to lake Maurepas, receiving in its courſe the river Amit, which is navigable for batteaux to a conſiderable diſtance.

Lake Maurepas is about ten miles in length, and ſeven in breadth ; and there is a paſſage of ſeven miles between this and Lake Pontchartrain.

Lake Pontchartrain is about forty miles long, twenty four broad, and eighteen feet deep. From this lake to the ſea the channel is ten miles long, and three hundred yards wide ; and the water deep enough to admit large veſſels through theſe lakes, and their communications. This place, if attended to, might be of conſequence to all the the weſtern country, and to the commerce of Weſt-Florida : For it may reaſonably be ſuppoſed, that the inhabitants and traders of the weſtern country would rather trade at this place than at New Orleans, if they could have as good returns for their peltry, and the produce of their ſoil, as it makes a conſiderable difference in their

voyage,

voyage, and faves labour, money and time. Experience will doubtlefs produce confiderable improvements, and render the navigation of the Miffiffippi, either by thefe lakes, or New Orleans, nearly as cheap as any other. That the Miffiffippi can anfwer every valuable purpofe of trade and commerce is proved already to a demonftration by experience.

I have reafon to believe that the time is not far diftant when New Orleans will be a great trading city, and perhaps another will be built near Mantchac, at Iberville, that may in time rival its glory.

A prodigious number of iflands, fome of which are of great extent, are interfperfed in that mighty river; and the difficulty in afcending it in the Spring when the floods are high, is compenfated by eddies or counter currents, which moftly run in the bends near the banks of the river with nearly equal velocity againft the ftream, and affift the afcending boats. This river is rapid in thofe parts which have clufters of iflands, fhoals and fand-banks; but the rapidity of thefe places will be no inconvenience to the newly invented mechanical boats,* it being their peculiar property to fail beft in fmart currents.

From

---

* *This plan is now in agitation in Virginia, and*

From New Orleans to the Falls of Ohio, batteaux, carrying about 40 tons, have been rowed
by eighteen or twenty men in eight or ten weeks,
which, at the extent, will not amount to more
than five hundred pounds expence, which experience has proved to be about one third of that
from Philadelphia. It is highly probable that in
time the distance will be exceedingly shortened by
cuting a-cross bends of the river.

Charlevoix relates, that at Coupee or Cut-point,
the river formerly made a great turn, and some
Canadians, by deepening the channel of a small
brook, diverted the waters of the river into it.
The impetuosity of the stream was so violent, and
the soil of so rich and loose a quality, that in a
short time the point was entirely cut through,
and the old channel left dry, except in inunda-
tions, by which travellers save 14 leagues of their
voyage.

recommended to government by two gentlemen of first
rate abilities, Mr. Charles Rumsey and Doct. James
M'Macken. Their proposals are, " to construct a
species of boat, of the burthen of ten tons, that shall
fail, or be propelled by the force of mechanical pow-
ers thereto applied, up the stream of a fresh water
river the distance of between 25 and 40 miles a
day, notwithstanding the velocity of the water should
move at the rate of 10 miles an hour, to be wrought
at no greater expence than that of three hands."

voyage. The new channel has been founded with a line of thirty fathoms without finding bottom. When the diftance is fhortened, which I believe may readily be done, and the mechanical boats brought to their higheft improvement, the expences of a voyage from New Orleans to the Falls of Ohio will be attended with inconfiderable expence. Now we know by experience that forty tons of goods cannot be taken to the Falls of Ohio from Philadelphia under fixteen hundred pounds expence ; but by improvements on the Miffiffippi, with the conveniences of thefe boats, goods can be brought from New Orleans to the Falls for the tenth part of that expence ; and if they are fold at one hundred pounds per cent. now, when brought from Philadelphia at expences fo great, what may the merchant afford to fell his goods at, who brings them fo much cheaper ? Befides, the great advantages arifing from the exporting of peltry, and country produce, which never can be conveyed to the eaftern ports to any advantage. It is evident alfo that the market from which they receive imports, muft confequently receive their exports, which is the only return they can poffibly make.

By ftating the commerce of Kentucke in its proper terms, we find the expences fuch, that we conclude with propriety, that that country will be

be fupplied with goods as cheap as if fituated but forty miles from Philadelphia.

But perhaps it will be replied, New Orleans is in the poffeffion of the Spaniards, who, whenever they pleafe, may make ufe of that fort, and fome others they have on the Miffiffippi, to prevent the navigation, and ruin the trade. The paffage through Iberville is alfo fubject to the Spaniards, and befides, inconvenient ; that ftream continuing fo fhort a time, and in the moft difadvantageous feafon.

I grant it will be abfurd to expect a free navigation of the Miffiffippi whilft the Spaniards are in poffeffion of New Orleans. To fuppofe it, is an idea calculated to impofe only upon the weak. They may perhaps trade with us upon their own terms, while they think it confiftent with their intereft,* but no friendfhip in trade exifts when intereft expires ; therefore, when the weftern country becomes populous and ripe for trade, found policy tells us the Floridas muft be ours too. According to the articles of the Definitive Treaty, we are to have a free and unmolefted navigation
of

---

* *Article 8th of the late Definitive Treaty, fays, The navigation of the Miffiffippi River from its fource to the ocean, fhall for ever remain free and open to the fubjects of Great-Britain and the citizens of the United States.*

of the Miſſiſſippi; but experience teaches mankind that treaties are not always to be depended
on, the moſt ſolemn being broken. Hence
we learn that no one ſhould put much faith in
any ſtate; and the trade and commerce of the
Miſſiſſippi River cannot be ſo well ſecured in
any other poſſeſſion as our own.

Although the Iberville only admits of a ſhort
and inconvenient navigation, yet if a commercial
town were built there, it would be the center of
the weſtern trade; and a land carriage of ten or
twelve miles would be counted no diſadvantage
to the merchant. Nay, I doubt not, that in time
a canal will be broke through the gut of Iberville,
which may divert the water of Miſſiſſippi that
way, and render it a place of the greateſt conſequence in America; but this important period
is reſerved for futurity.

APPENDIX:

APPENDIX.

The ADVENTURES of Col. DA-
NIEL BOON; containing a NARRA-
TIVE of the WARS of Kentucke.

CURIOSITY is natural to the foul of
man, and interefting objects have a powerful influence on our affections. Let thefe influ-
encing powers actuate, by the permiffion or
difpofal of Providence, from felfish or focial views,
yet in time the myfterious will of Heaven is un-
folded, and we behold our conduct, from whatfoever motives excited, operating to anfwer the important defigns of heaven. Thus we behold Kentucke, lately an howling wildernefs, the habitation of
favages and wild beafts, become a fruitful field;
this region, fo favourably diftinguifhed by nature, now become the habitation of civilization,

G

at

at a period unparalleled in hiſtory, in the midſt of a raging war, and under all the diſadvantages of emigration to a country ſo remote from the inhabited parts of the continent. Here, where the hand of violence ſhed the blood of the innocent ; where the horrid yells of ſavages, and the groans of the diſtreſſed, founded in our ears, we now hear the praiſes and adorations of our Creator ; where wretched wigwams ſtood, the miſerable abodes of ſavages, we behold the foundations of cities laid, that, in all probability, will rival the glory of the greateſt upon earth. And we view Kentucke ſituated on the fertile banks of the great Ohio, riſing from obſcurity to ſhine with ſplendor, equal to any other of the ſtars of the American hemiſphere.

The ſettling of this region well deſerves a place in hiſtory. Moſt of the memorable events I have myſelf been exerciſed in ; and, for the ſatisfaction of the public, will briefly relate the circumſtances of my adventures, and ſcenes of life, from my firſt movement to this country until this day.

It was on the firſt of May, in the year 1769, that I reſigned my domeſtic happineſs for a time, and left my family and peaceable habitation on the Yadkin River, in North-Carolina, to wander through the wilderneſs of America, in queſt of the

the country of Kentucke, in company with John
Finley, John Stewart, Joseph Holden, James
Monay, and William Cool. We proceeded fuc-
cefsfully, and after a long and fatiguing journey
through a mountainous wildernefs, in a weftward direction, on the feventh day of June following, we found ourfelves on Red-River, where
John Finley had for merly been trading with
the Indians, and, from the top of an eminence,
faw with pleafure the beautiful level of Kentucke. Here let me obferve, that for fome time we
had experienced the moft uncomfortable weather as a prelibation of our future fufferings. At
this place we encamped, and made a fhelter to defend us from the inclement feafon, and began to
hunt and reconnoitre the country. We found e-
very where abundance of wild beafts of all forts,
through this vaft foreft. The buffaloes were
more frequent than I have feen cattle in the fettlements, browzing on the leaves of the cane, or
croping the herbage on thofe extenfive plains, fear-
lefs, becaufe ignorant, of the violence of man.
Sometimes we faw hundreds in a drove, and the
numbers about the falt fprings were amazing.
In this foreft, the habitation of beafts of every
kind natural to America, we practifed hunting
with great fuccefs until the twenty-fecond day of
December following.

This day John Stewart and I had a pleafing
ramble,

ramble, but fortune changed the fcene in the clofe of it. We had paffed through a great foreft, on which ftood myriads of trees, fome gay with bloffoms, others rich with fruits. Nature was here a feries of wonders, and a fund of delight. Here fhe difplayed her ingenuity and induftry in a variety of flowers and fruits, beautifully coloured, elegantly fhaped, and charmingly flavoured ; and we were diverted with innumerable animals prefenting themfelves perpetually to our view.—In the decline of the day, near Kentucke river, as we afcended the brow of a fmall hill, a number of Indians rufhed out of a thick cane-brake upon us, and made us prifoners. The time of our forrow was now arrived, and the fcene fully opened. The Indians plundered us of what we had, and kept us in confinement feven days, treating us with common favage ufage. During this time we difcovered no uneafinefs or defire to efcape, which made them lefs fufpicious of us ; but in the dead of night, as we lay in a thick cane-brake by a large fire, when fleep had locked up their fenfes, my fituation not difpofing me for reft, I touched my companion and gently awoke him. We improved this favourable opportunity, and departed, leaving them to take their reft, and fpeedily directed our courfe towards our old camp, but found it plundered, and the company difperfed and gone home. About this time my

my brother, Squire Boon, with another adventurer, who came to explore the country shortly
after us, was wandering through the foreft, determined to find me, if poffible, and accidentally
found our camp. Notwithftanding the unfortunate circumftances of our company, and our dangerous fituation, as furrounded with hoftile fa-
favages, our meeting fo fortunately in the wildernefs made us reciprocally fenfible of the utmoft
fatisfaction. So much does friendfhip triumph
over misfortune, that forrows and fufferings va-
nifh at the meeting not only of real friends, but
of the moft diftant acquaintances, and fubftitutes
happinefs in their room.

Soon after this, my companion in captivity,
John Stewart, was killed by the favages, and
the man that came with my brother returned
home by himfelf. We were then in a dangerous,
helplefs fituation, expofed daily to perils and
death amongft favages and wild beafts, not a
white man in the country but ourfelves.
Thus fituated, many hundred miles from our
families in the howling wildernefs, I believe few
would have equally enjoyed the happinefs we experienced. I often obferved to my brother, You
fee now how little nature requires to be fatisfied.
Felicity, the companion of content, is rather
found in our own breafts than in the enjoyment
of external things: And I firmly believe it requires

quires but a little philofophy to make a man happy in whatfoever ftate he is. This confifts in a full refignation to the will of Providence; and a refigned foul finds pleafure in a path ftrewed with briars and thorns.

We continued not in a ftate of indolence, but hunted every day, and prepared a little cottage to defend us from the Winter ftorms. We remained there undifturbed during the Winter; and on the firft day of May, 1770, my brother returned home to the fettlement by himfelf, for a new recruit of horfes and ammunition, leaving me by myfelf, without bread, falt or fugar, without company of my fellow creatures, or even a horfe or dog. I confefs I never before was under greater neceffity of exercifing philofophy and fortitude. A few days I paffed uncomfortably. The idea of a beloved wife and family, and their anxiety upon the account of my abfence and expofed fituation, made fenfible impreffions on my heart. A thoufand dreadful apprehenfions prefented themfelves to my view, and had undoubtedly difpofed me to melancholy, if further indulged.

One day I undertook a tour through the country, and the diverfity and beauties of nature I met with in this charming feafon, expelled every gloomy and vexatious thought. Juft at the clofe

of

of day the gentle gales retired, and left the place to the difpofal of a profound calm. Not a breeze fhook the moft tremulous leaf. I had gained the fummit of a commanding ridge, and, looking round with aftonifhing delight, beheld the ample plains, the beauteous tracts below. On the other hand, I furveyed the famous river Ohio that rolled in filent dignity, marking the weftern boundary of Kentucke with inconceivable grandeur. At a vaft diftance I beheld the mountains lift their venerable brows, and penetrate the clouds. All things were ftill. I kindled a fire near a fountain of fweet water, and feafted on the loin of a buck, which a few hours before I had killed. The fullen fhades of night foon overfpread the whole hemifphere, and the earth feemed to gafp after the hovering moifture. My roving excurfion this day had fatigued my body, and diverted my imagination. I laid me down to fleep, and I awoke not until the fun had chafed away the night. I continued this tour, and in a few days explored a confiderable part of the country, each day equally pleafed as the firft. I returned again to my old camp, which was not difturbed in my abfence. I did not confine my lodging to it, but often repofed in thick cane-brakes, to avoid the favages, who, I believe, often vifited my camp, but fortunately for me, in my abfence. In this fituation I was conftantly expofed to danger, and death. How unhappy fuch a fituation for

a man

a man tormented with fear, which is vain if no danger comes, and if it does, only augments the pain. It was my happiness to be destitute of this afflicting passion, with which I had the greatest reason to be affected. The prowling wolves diverted my nocturnal hours with perpetual howlings; and the various species of animals in this vast forest, in the day time, were continually in my view.

Thus I was surrounded with plenty in the midst of want. I was happy in the midst of dangers and inconveniences. In such a diversity it was impossible I should be disposed to melancholy. No populous city, with all the varieties of commerce and stately structures, could afford so much pleasure to my mind, as the beauties of nature I found here.

Thus, through an uninterrupted scene of sylvan pleasures, I spent the time until the 27th day of July following, when my brother, to my great felicity, met me, according to appointment, at our old camp. Shortly after, we left this place, not thinking it safe to stay there longer, and proceeded to Cumberland river, reconnoitring that part of the country until March, 1771, and giving names to the different waters.

Soon after, I returned home to my family with a determination to bring them as soon as possible

poffible to live in Kentucke, which I efteemed a fecond paradife, at the rifk of my life and fortune.

I returned fafe to my old habitation, and found my family in happy circumftances. I fold my farm on the Yadkin, and what goods we could not carry with us; and on the twenty-fifth day of September, 1773, bade a farewel to our friends, and proceeded on our journey to Kentucke, in company with five families more, and forty men that joined us in Powel's Valley, which is one hundred and fifty miles from the now fettled parts of Kentucke. This promifing beginning was foon overcaft with a cloud of adverfity; for upon the tenth day of October, the rear of our company was attacked by a number of Indians, who killed fix, and wounded one man. Of thefe my eldeft fon was one that fell in the action. Though we defended ourfelves, and repulfed the enemy, yet this unhappy affair fcattered our cattle, brought us into extreme difficulty, and fo difcouraged the whole company, that we retreated forty miles, to the fettlement on Clench river. We had paffed over two mountains, viz. Powel's and Walden's, and were approaching Cumberland mountain when this adverfe fortune overtook us. Thefe mountains are in the wildernefs, as we pafs from the old fettlements in Virginia to Kentucke, are ranged in a S. weft and

H   N. eaft

N. eaft direction, are of a great length and breadth, and not far diftant from each other. Over thefe, nature hath formed paffes, that are lefs difficult than might be expected from a view of fuch huge piles. The afpect of thefe cliffs is fo wild and horrid, that it is impoffible to behold them without terror. The fpectator is apt to imagine that nature had formerly fuffered fome violent convulfion; and that thefe are the difmembered remains of the dreadful fhock; the ruins, not of Perfepolis or Palmyra, but of the world!

I remained with my family on Clench until the fixth of June, 1774, when I and one Michael Stoner were folicited by Governor Dunmore, of Virginia, to go to the Falls of the Ohio to conduct into the fettlement a number of furveyors that had been fent thither by him fome months before; this country having about this time drawn the attention of many adventurers. We immediately complied with the Governor's requeft, and conducted in the furveyors, compleating a tour of eight hundred miles, through many difficulties, in fixty-two days.

Soon after I returned home, I was ordered to take the command of three garrifons during the campaign, which Governor Dunmore carried on againft the Shawanefe Indians: After the conclufion of which, the Militia was difcharged from each

each garrifon, and I being relieved from my poft, was folicited by a number of North-Carolina gentlemen, that were about purchafing the lands lying on the S. fide of Kentucke River, from the Cherokee Indians, to attend their treaty at Wataga, in March, 1775, to negotiate with them, and, mention the boundaries of the purchafe. This I accepted, and at the requeft of the fame gentlemen, undertook to mark out a road in the beft paffage from the fettlement through the wildernefs to Kentucke, with fuch affiftance as I thought neceffary to employ for fuch an important undertaking.

I foon began this work, having collected a number of enterprifing men, well armed We proceeded with all poffible expedition until we came within fifteen miles of where Boonfborough now ftands, and where we were fired upon by a party of Indians that killed two, and wounded two of our number; yet, although furprifed and taken at a difadvantage, we ftood our ground. This was on the twentieth of March, 17 5. Three days after, we were fired upon again, and had two men killed, and three wounded. Afterwards we proceeded on to Kentucke river without oppofition; and on the fi ft day of April began to erect the fort of Boonfborough at a falt lick, about fixty yards from the river, on the S. fide.

On

On the fourth day, the Indians killed one of our men.——We were bufily employed in building this fort, until the fourteenth day of June following, without any farther oppofition from the Indians; and having finifhed the works, I returned to my family, on Clench.

In a fhort time, I proceeded to remove my family from Clench to this garrifon; where we arrived fafe without any other difficulties than fuch as are common to this paffage, my wife and daughter being the firft white women that ever ftood on the banks of Kentucke river.

On the twenty-fourth day of December following we had one man killed, and one wounded, by the Indians, who feemed determined to perfecute us for erecting this fortification.

On the fourteenth day of July, 1776, two of Col. Calaway's daughters, and one of mine, were taken prifoners near the fort. I immediately purfued the Indians, with only eight men, and on the fixteenth overtook them, killed two of the party, and recovered the girls. The fame day on which this attempt was made, the Indians divided themfelves into different parties, and attacked feveral forts, which were fhortly before this time erected, doing a great deal of mifchief. This was extremely diftreffing to the new fettlers. The

innocent

innocent hufbandman was fhot down, while bu-
fy cultivating the foil for his family's fupply.
Moft of the cattle around the ftations were deftroyed. They continued their hoftilities in this
manner until the fifteenth of April, 1777, when
they attacked Boonfborough with a party of a-
bove one hundred in number, killed one man,
and wounded four.—Their lofs in this attack was
not certainly known to us.

On the fourth day of July following, a party
of about two hundred Indians attacked Boonfborough, killed one man, and wounded two.
They befieged us forty-eight hours; during
which time feven of them were killed, and at
laft, finding themfelves not likely to prevail, they
raifed the fiege, and departed.

The Indians had difpofed their warriors in different parties at this time, and attacked the different garrifons to prevent their affifting each
other, and did much injury to the diftreffed inhabitants.

On the nineteenth day of this month, Col.
Logan's fort was befieged by a party of about
two hundred Indians. During this dreadful fiege
they did a great deal of mifchief, diftreffed the
garrifon, in which were only fifteen men, killed
two, and wounded one. The enemies lofs was
uncertain,

uncertain, from the common practice which the Indians have of carrying off their dead in time of battle. Col. Harrod's fort was then defended by only sixty-five men, and Boonsborough by twenty-two, there being no more forts or white men in the country, except at the Falls, a confiderable diftance from thefe, and all taken collectively, were but a handful to the numerous warriors that were every where difperfed through the country, intent upon doing all the mifchief that favage barbarity could invent. Thus we paffed through a fcene of fufferings that exceeds defcription.

On the twenty-fifth of this month a reinforcement of forty-five men arrived from North-Carolina, and about the twentieth of Auguft following, Col. Bowman arrived with one hundred men from Virginia. Now we began to ftrengthen, and from hence, for the fpace of fix weeks, we had fkirmifhes with Indians, in one quarter or other, almoft every day.

The favages now learned the fuperiority of the Long Knife, as they call the Virginians, by experience; being out-generalled in almoft every battle. Our affairs began to wear a new afpect, and the enemy, not daring to venture on open war, practifed fecret michief at times.

On

On the firſt day of January, 1778, I went with a party of thirty men to the Blue Licks, on Licking River, to make ſalt for the different garriſons in the country.

On the ſeventh day of February, as I was hunting, to procure meat for the company, I met with a party of one hundred and two Indians, and two Frenchmen, on their march againſt Boonſborough, that place being particularly the object of the enemy.

They purſued, and took me ; and brought me on the eighth day to the Licks, where twenty-ſeven of my party were, three of them having previouſly returned home with the ſalt. I knowing it was impoſſible for them to eſcape, capitulated with the enemy, and, at a diſtance in their view, gave notice to my men of their ſituation, with orders not to reſiſt, but ſurrender themſelves captives.

The generous uſage the Indians had promiſed before in my capitulation, was afterwards fully complied with, and we proceeded with them as priſoners to old Chelicothe, the principal Indian town, on Little Miami, where we arrived, after an uncomfortable journey, in very ſevere weather, on the eighteenth day of February, and received as good treatment as priſoners could expect from ſavages.

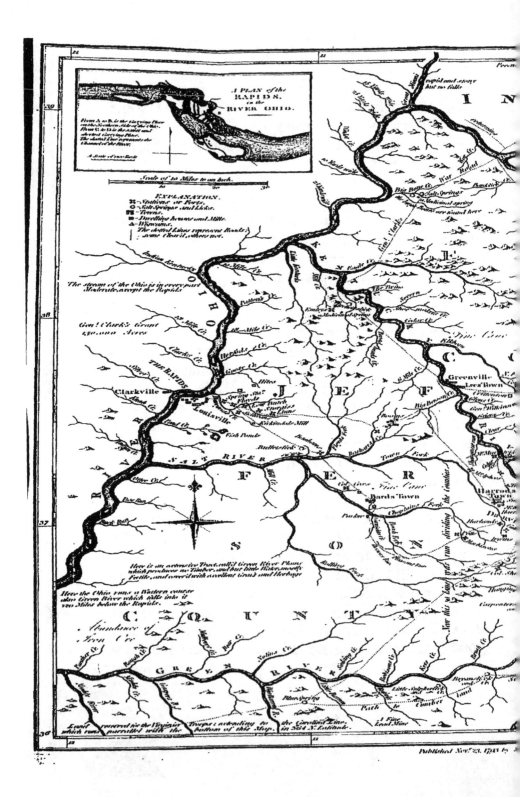

A PLAN of the RAPIDS in the RIVER OHIO

Scale of 10 Miles to an inch.

EXPLANATION.
Stations or Forts.
Salt Springs and Licks.
Towns.
Dwelling houses and Mills.
Mountains.
The dotted lines represent Roads; some Clear'd, others not.

Published Nov.r 23. 1784 by

into a family where I became a fon, and had a great fhare in the affection of my new parents, brothers, fifters, and friends. I was exceedingly familiar and friendly with them, always appearing as chearful and fatisfied as poffible, and they put great confidence in me. I often went a hunting with them, and frequently gained their applaufe for my activity at our fhooting-matches. I was careful not to exceed many of them in fhooting; for no people are more envious than they in this fport. I could obferve, in their countenances and geftures, the greateft expreffions of joy when they exceeded me; and, when the reverfe happened, of envy. The Shawanefe king took great notice of me, and treated me with profound refpect, and entire friendfhip, often entrufting me to hunt at my liberty. I frequently returned with the fpoils of the woods, and as often prefented fome of what I had taken to him, expreffive of duty to my fovereign. My food and lodging was, in common, with them, not fo good indeed as I could defire, but neceffity made every thing acceptable.

I now began to meditate an efcape, and carefully avoided their fufpicions, continuing with them at Old Chelicothe until the firft day of June following, and then was taken by them to the falt fprings on Sciotha, and kept there, making falt, ten days. During this time I hunted

I   fome

ſome for them, and found the land, for a great extent about this river, to exceed the ſoil of Kentucke, if poſſible, and remarkably well watered.

When I returned to Chelicothe, alarmed to ſee four hundred and fifty Indians, of their choiceſt warriors, painted and armed in a fearful manner, ready to march againſt Boonſborough, I determined to eſcape the firſt opportunity.

On the ſixteenth, before ſun-riſe, I departed in the moſt ſecret manner, and arrived at Boonſborough on the twentieth, after a journey of one hundred and ſixty miles; during which, I had but one meal.

I found our fortreſs in a bad ſtate of defence, but we proceeded immediately to repair our flanks, ſtrengthen our gates and poſterns, and form double baſtions, which we compleated in ten days. In this time we daily expected the arrival of the Indian army ; and at length, one of my fellow priſoners, eſcaping from them, arrived, informing us that the enemy had an account of my departure, and poſtponed their expedition three weeks.—The Indians had ſpies out viewing our movements, and were greatly alarmed with our increaſe in number and fortifications. The Grand Councils of the nations were held frequently, and with more deliberation than uſual. They evidently

dently faw the approaching hour when the Long Knife would difpoffefs them of their defirable habitations; and anxioufly concerned for futurity, determined utterly to extirpate the whites out of Kentucke. We were not intimidated by their movements, but frequently gave them proofs of our courage.

About the firft of Auguft, I made an incurfion into the Indian country, with a party of nineteen men, in order to furprife a fmall town up Sciotha, called Paint-Creek-Town. We advanced within four miles thereof, where we met a party of thirty Indians, on their march againft Boonfborough, intending to join the others from Chelicothe. A fmart fight enfued betwixt us for fome time : At length the favages gave way, and fled. We had no lofs on our fide : The enemy had one killed, and two wounded. We took from them three horfes, and all their baggage ; and being informed, by two of our number that went to their town, that the Indians had entirely evacuated it, we proceeded no further, and returned with all poffible expedition to affift our garrifon againft the other party. We paffed by them on the fixth day, and on the feventh, we arrived fafe at Boonfborough.

On the eighth, the Indian army arrived, being four hundred and forty-four in number, commanded
by

by Capt. Duquefne, eleven other Frenchmen, and fome of their own chiefs, and marched up within view of our fort, with Britifh and French colours flying; and having fent a fummons to me, in his Britannick Majefty's name, to furrender the fort, I requefted two days confideration, which was granted.

It was now a critical period with us.—We were a fmall number in the garrifon.—A powerful army before our walls, whofe appearance proclaimed inevitable death, fearfully painted, and marking their footfteps with defolation. Death was preferable to captivity; and if taken by ftorm, we muft inevitably be devoted to deftruction. In this fituation we concluded to maintain our garrifon, if poffible. We immediately proceeded to collect what we could of our horfes, and other cattle, and bring them through the pofterns into the fort: And in the evening of the ninth, I returned anfwer, that we were determined to defend our fort while a man was living.—Now, faid I to their commander, who ftood attentively hearing my fentiments, We laugh at all your formidable preparations: But thank you for giving us notice and time to provide for our defence. Your efforts will not prevail; for our gates fhall for ever deny you admittance.—Whether this anfwer affected their courage, or not, I cannot tell; but, contrary to our expectations, they

formed

formed a fcheme to deceive us, declaring it was their orders, from Governor Hamilton, to take us captives, and not to deftroy us; but if nine of us would come out, and treat with them, they would immediatly withdraw their forces from our walls, and return home peaceably. This founded grateful in our ears; and we agreed to the propofal.

We held the treaty within fixty yards of the garrifon, on purpofe to divert them from a breach of honour, as we could not avoid fufpicions of the favages. In this fituation the articles were formally agreed to, and figned; and the Indians told us it was cuftomary with them, on fuch occafions, for two Indians to fhake hands with every white-man in the treaty, as an evidence of entire friendfhip. We agreed to this alfo, but were foon convinced their policy was to take us prifoners.—They immediately grappled us; but, although furrounded by hundreds of favages, we extricated ourfelves from them, and efcaped all fafe into the garrifon, except one that was wounded, through a heavy fire from their army. They immediately attacked us on every fide, and a conftant heavy fire enfued between us day and night for the fpace of nine days.

In this time the enemy began to undermine our fort, which was fituated fixty yards from Kentucke

tucke river. They began at the water-mark, and proceeded in the bank fome diftance, which we underftood by their making the water muddy with the clay; and we immediately proceeded to difappoint their defign, by cutting a trench a-crofs their fubterranean paffage. The enemy difcovering our counter-mine, by the clay we threw out of the fort, defifted from that ftratagem: And experience now fully convincing them that neither their power nor policy could effect their purpofe, on the twentieth day of Auguft they raifed the fiege, and departed.

During this dreadful fiege, which threatened death in every form, we had two men killed, and four wounded, befides a number of cattle. We killed of the enemy thirty-feven, and wounded a great number. After they were gone, we picked up one hundred and twenty-five pounds weight of bullets, befides what ftuck in the logs of our fort; which certainly is a great proof of their induftry. Soon after this, I went into the fettlement, and nothing worthy of a place in this account paffed in my affairs for fome time.

During my abfence from Kentucke, Col. Bowman carried on an expedition againft the Shawanefe, at Old Chelicothe, with one hundred and fixty men, in July, 1779. Here they arrived undifcovered, and a battle enfued, which lafted until
.til

til ten o'clock, A. M. when Col. Bowman, finding he could not fucceed at this time, retreated about thirty miles. The Indians, in the mean time, collecting all their forces, purfued and overtook him, when a fmart fight continued near two hours, not to the advantage of Col. Bowman's party.

Col. Harrod propofed to mount a number of horfe, and furioufly to rufh upon the favages, who at this time fought with remarkable fury. This defperate ftep had a happy effect, broke their line of battle, and the favages fled on all fides. In thefe two battles we had nine killed, and one wounded. The enemy's lofs uncertain, only two fcalps being taken.

On the twenty-fecond day of June, 1780, a large party of Indians and Canadians, about fix hundred in number, commanded by Col. Bird, attacked Riddle's and Martin's ftations, at the Forks of Licking River, with fix pieces of artillery. They carried this expedition fo fecretly, that the unwary inhabitants did not difcover them, until they fired upon the forts; and, not being prepared to oppofe them, were obliged to furrender themfelves miferable captives to barbarous favages, who immediately after tomahawked one man and two women, and loaded all the others with heavy baggage, forcing them along
toward

toward their towns, able or unable to march. Such as were weak and faint by the way, they tomahawked. The tender women, and helpless children, fell victims to their cruelty. This, and the savage treatment they received afterwards, is shocking to humanity, and too barbarous to relate.

The hostile disposition of the savages, and their allies, caused General Clark, the commandant at the Falls of the Ohio, immediately to begin an expedition with his own regiment, and the armed force of the country, against Pecaway, the principal town of the Shawanese, on a branch of Great Miami, which he finished with great success, took seventeen scalps, and burnt the town to ashes, with the loss of seventeen men.

About this time I returned to Kentucke with my family; and here, to avoid an enquiry into my conduct, the reader being before informed of my bringing my family to Kentucke, I am under the necessity of informing him that, during my captivity with the Indians, my wife, who despaired of ever seeing me again, expecting the Indians had put a period to my life, oppressed with the distresses of the country, and bereaved of me, her only happiness, had, before I returned, transported my family and goods, on horses, through the wilderness, amidst a multitude of dangers, to her father's house, in North-Carolina.

Shortly

Shortly after the troubles at Boonfborough, I went to them, and lived peaceably there until this time. The hiftory of my going home, and returning with my family, forms a feries of difficulties, an account of which would fwell a volume, and being foreign to my purpofe, I fhall purpofely omit them.

I fettled my family in Boonfborough once more; and fhortly after, on the fixth day of October, 1780, I went in company with my brother to the Blue Licks; and, on our return home, we were fired upon by a party of Indians. They fhot him, and purfued me, by the fcent of their dog, three miles; but I killed the dog, and efcaped. The Winter foon came on, and was very fevere,. which confined the Indians to their wigwams.

The feverity of this Winter caufed great difficulties in Kentucke. The enemy had deftroyed moft of the corn, the Summer before. This neceffary article was fcarce, and dear; and the inhabitants lived chiefly on the flefh of buffaloes. The circumftances of many were very lamentable: However, being a hardy race of people, and accuftomed to difficulties and neceffities, they were wonderfully fupported through all their fufferings, until the enfuing Fall, when we received abundance from the fertile foil.

K.   Towards

Towards Spring, we were frequently haraſſed by Indians; and, in May, 1782, a party aſſaulted Aſhton's ſtation, killed one man, and took a Negro priſoner. Capt. Aſhton, with twenty-five men, purſued, and overtook the ſavages, and a ſmart fight enſued, which laſted two hours; but they being ſuperior in number, obliged Captain Aſhton's party to retreat, with the loſs of eight killed, and four mortally wounded; their brave commander himſelf being numbered among the dead.

The Indians continued their hoſtilities; and, about the tenth of Auguſt following, two boys were taken from Major Hoy's ſtation. This party was purſued by Capt. Holder and ſeventeen men, who were alſo defeated, with the loſs of four men killed, and one wounded. Our affairs became more and more alarming. Several ſtations which had lately been erected in the country were continually infeſted with ſavages, ſtealing their horſes and killing the men at every opportunity. In a field, near Lexington, an Indian ſhot a man, and running to ſcalp him, was himſelf ſhot from the fort, and fell dead upon his enemy.

Every day we experienced recent miſchiefs. The barbarous ſavage nations of Shawaneſe, Cherokees, Wyandots, Tawas, Delawares, and ſeveral others near Detroit, united in a war againſt us, us, and affembled their choiceft warriors at old Chelicothe, to go on the expedition, in order to deftroy us, and entirely depopulate the country. Their favage minds were inflamed to mifchief by two abandoned men, Captains M'Kee and Girty. Thefe led them to execute every diabolical fcheme; and, on the fifteenth day of Auguft, commanded a party of Indians and Canadians, of about five hundred, in number, againft Briant's ftation, five miles from Lexington. Without demanding a furrender, they furioufly affaulted the garrifon, which was happily prepared to oppofe them; and, after they had expended much ammunition in vain, and killed the cattle round the fort, not being likely to make themfelves mafters of this place, they raifed the fiege, and departed in the morning of the third day after they came, with the lofs of about thirty killed, and the number of wounded uncertain.—Of the garrifon four were killed, and three wounded.

On the eighteenth day Col. Todd, Col. Trigg, Major Harland, and myfelf, fpeedily collected one hundred and feventy-fix men, well armed, and purfued the favages. They had marched beyond the Blue Licks to a remarkable bend of the main fork of Licking River, about forty-three miles from Lexington, as it is particularly reprefented in the map, where we overtook them on the

the nineteenth day. The favages obferving us, gave way; and we, being ignorant of their numbers, paffed the river. When the enemy faw our proceedings, having greatly the advantage of us in fituation, they formed the line of battle, as reprefented in the map, from one bend of Licking to the other, about a mile from the Blue Licks. An exceeding fierce battle immediately began, for about fifteen minutes, when we, being over-powered by numbers, were obliged to retreat, with the lofs of fixty-feven men; feven of whom were taken prifoners. The brave and much lamented Colonels Todd and Trigg, Major Harland and my fecond fon, were among the dead. We were informed that the Indians, numbering their dead, found they had four killed more than we; and therefore, four of the prifoners they had taken, were, by general confent, ordered to be killed, in a moft barbarous manner, by the young warriors, in order to train them up to cruelty; and then they proceeded to their towns.

On our retreat we were met by Col. Logan, haftening to join us, with a number of well armed men. This powerful affiftance we unfortunately wanted in the battle; for, notwithftanding the enemy's fuperiority of numbers, they acknowledged that, if they had received one more fire from us, they fhould undoubtedly have given way. So valiantly did our fmall party fight, that,

that, to the memory of thofe who unfortunately fell in the battle, enough of honour cannot
be paid. Had Col. Logan and his party been
with us, it is highly probable we fhould have
given the favages a total defeat.

I cannot reflect upon this dreadful fcene, but
forrow fills my heart. A zeal for the defence of
their country led thefe heroes to the fcene of action, though with a few men to attack a powerful army of experienced warriors. When we
gave way, they purfued us with the utmoft ea-
gernefs, and in every quarter fpread deftruction.
The river was difficult to crofs, and many were
killed in the flight, fome juft entering the river,
fome in the water, others after croffing in afcending the cliffs. Some efcaped on horfe-back, a
few on foot; and, being difperfed every where,
in a few hours, brought the melancholy news of
this unfortunate battle to Lexington. Many wi-
dows were now made. The reader may guefs
what forrow filled the hearts of the inhabitants,
exceeding any thing that I am able to defcribe.
Being reinforced, we returned to bury the dead,
and found their bodies ftrewed every where, cut
and mangled in a dreadful manner. This mourn-
ful fcene exhibited a horror almoft unparalleled:
Some torn and eaten by wild beafts; thofe in the
river eaten by fifhes; all in fuch a putrified condition,

dition, that no one could be diftinguifhed from another.

As foon as General Claik, then at the Falls of the Ohio, who was ever our ready friend, and merits the love and gratitude of all his country-men, underftood the circumftances of this unfortunate action, he ordered an expedition, with all poffible hafte, to purfue the favages, which was fo expeditioufly effected, that we overtook them within two miles of their towns, and probably might have obtained a great victory, had not two of their number met us about two hundred poles before we come up. Thefe returned quick as lightening to their camp with the alarming news of a mighty army in view. The favages fled in the utmoft diforder, evacuated their towns, and reluctantly left their territory to our mercy. We immediately took poffeffion of Old Chelicothe without oppofition, being deferted by its inhabitants. We continued our purfuit through five towns on the Miami rivers, Old Chelicothe, Pecaway, New Chelicothe, Will's Towns, and Chelicothe, burnt them all to afhes, entirely deftroyed their corn, and other fruits, and every where fpread a fcene of defolation in the country. In this expedition we took feven prifoners and five fcalps, with the lofs of only four men, two of whom were accidentally killed by our own army.

This

This campaign in some measure damped the spirits of the Indians, and made them sensible of our superiority. Their connections were dissolved, their armies scattered, and a future invasion put entirely out of their power; yet they continued to practife mischief secretly upon the inhabitants, in the exposed parts of the country.

In October following, a party made an excursion into that district called the Crab Orchard, and one of them, being advanced some distance before the others, boldly entered the house of a poor defenceless family, in which was only a Negro man, a woman and her children, terrified with the apprehensions of immediate death. The savage, perceiving their defenceless situation, without offering violence to the family attempted to captivate the Negro, who, happily proved an over-match for him, threw him on the ground, and, in the struggle, the mother of the children drew an ax from a corner of the cottage, and cut his head off, while her little daughter shut the door. The savages instantly appeared, and applied their tomahawks to the door. An old rusty gun-barrel, without a lock, lay in a corner, which the mother put through a small crevice, and the savages, perceiving it, fled. In the mean time, the alarm spread through the neighbourhood; the armed men collected immediately, and pursued the ravagers into the wilderness. Thus
Providence,

Providence, by the means of this Negro, saved the whole of the poor family from deſtruction. From that time, until the happy return of peace between the United States and Great-Britain, the Indians did us no miſchief. Finding the great king beyond the water diſappointed in his expectations, and conſcious of the importance of the Long Knife, and their own wretchedneſs, ſome of the nations immediately deſired peace; to which, at preſent, they ſeem univerſally diſpoſed, and are ſending ambaſſadors to General Clark, at the Falls of the Ohio, with the minutes of their Councils; a ſpecimen of which, in the minutes of the Piankaſhaw Council, is ſubjoined.

To conclude, I can now ſay that I have verified the ſaying of an old Indian who ſigned Col. Henderſon's deed. Taking me by the hand, at the delivery thereof, Brother, ſays he, we have given you a fine land, but I believe you will have much trouble in ſettling it.—My footſteps have often been marked with blood, and therefore I can truly ſubſcribe to its original name. Two darling ſons, and a brother, have I loſt by ſavage hands, which have alſo taken from me forty valuable horſes, and abundance of cattle. Many dark and ſleepleſs nights have I been a companion for owls, ſeparated from the chearful ſociety of men, ſcorched by the Summer's ſun, and
pinched

pinched by the Winter's cold, an instrument ordained to settle the wilderness. But now the scene is changed. Peace crowns the sylvan shade.

What thanks, what ardent and ceaseless thanks are due to that all-superintending Providence which has turned a cruel war into peace, brought order out of confusion, made the fierce savages placid, and turned away their hostile weapons from our country! May the same Almighty Goodness banish the accursed monster, war, from all lands, with her hated associates, rapine and insatiable ambition. Let peace, descending from her native heaven, bid her olives spring amidst the joyful nations; and plenty, in league with commerce, scatter blessings from her copious hand.

This account of my adventures will inform the reader of the most remarkable events of this country.—How I have in peace and safety, enjoying the sweets of liberty, and the bounties of Providence, with my once fellow-sufferers, in this delightful country, which I have seen purchased with a vast expence of blood and treasure, delighting in the prospect of its being, in a short time, one of the most opulent and powerful states on the continent of North-America; and which, with the love and gratitude of my country men,

L

Sorry:
The defect on the previous page was that way in the original book we reproduced.

I esteem a sufficient reward for all my toil and dangers.

DANIEL BOON.

Fayette county, Kentucke.

PIANKASHAW COUNCIL.

In a COUNCIL, *held with the Piankashaw Indians, by Thomas J. Dalton, at Post St. Vincent's, April* 15, 1784.

MY CHILDREN,

WHAT I have often told you, is now come to pass. This day I received news from my Great Chief, at the Falls of Ohio. Peace is made with the enemies of America. The White Flesh, the Americans, French, Spaniards, Dutch and English, this day smoke out

of

of the peace-pipe. The tomahawk is buried, and they are now friends.

I am told the Shawanese, Delawares, Chicasaws, Cherokees, and all other the Red Flesh, have taken the Long Knife by the hand. They have given up to them the prisoners that were in their nations.

My Children on Wabash,
Open your ears, and let what I tell you sink deep in your hearts. You know me. Near twenty years I have been among you. The Long Knife is my nation. I know their hearts; peace they carry in one hand, and war in the other.

I leave you to yourselves to judge. Consider, and now accept the one, or the other. We never beg peace of our enemies. If you love your women and children, receive the belt of wampum I present you. Return me my flesh you have in your villages, and the horses you stole from my people at Kentucke. Your corn-fields were never disturbed by the Long Knife. Your women and children lived quiet in their houses, while your warriors were killing and robbing my people. All this you know is the truth. This is the last time I shall speak to you. I have waited six moons to hear you speak, and to get my people from you. In ten nights I shall
leave

leave the Wabash ☐ &c. my Great Chief at the
Falls ☐ Ohio, whom I ☐ will be glad to hear,
from your own lips, what you have to say. Here
is tobacco I give you. Brother, ☐ consider what
I have said.—When I delivered the belt of blue
and white wampum, and said, Piankashaw,
speak ☐ ☐ ☐ to the Americans.

When the Piankashaw Chief answered;

My Great Father, the Long Knife,

You have been many years among us. You
have suffered by us. We still hope you will have
pity and compassion upon us, on our women
and children, the day is clear. The sun shines
on us; and the good news of peace appears in
our eyes. This day, my Father, this is the day
of ☐ ☐ the Wabash Indians. With one tongue
we ☐ speak.

We accept your peace belt. We return God
thanks ☐ ☐ ☐ the man that delivered us what
we ☐ long wished for, peace, with the White
people. My Father, we have many times counsel-
led ☐ ☐ you knew us; and you know how
times we deceived before.

We received the tomahawk from the English;
Powder forced us to it: We were attended by
other nations: We are sorry for it. We this
day called the bones of our friends that long a-
go were scattered upon the earth. We bury
them

them in one grave. We thus plant the tree of peace, that God may spread branches, so that we can all be secured from bad weather. They smoke as brothers out of the peace-pipe we now present you. Here, us, brother, is the pipe that gives us joy. Smoke out of it. Our warriors are glad you are the man we prefer it to. You see, Father, we have buried the tomahawk. We now make a green chain of friendship never to be broken; and to this, as our people, five is out of your pipe. My Father, you know it was angry with us for letting your traders and disturbing your people. He has given us hard, snow and cold weather, and God has cut off all your horses, with our own.

We are now a poor people. God, we hope, will help us; and our Father, the Long Knife, will have pity and compassion on our women and children. Poor flesh, my brother, is well that is among us, we shall collect them all together when they come in from hunting. Don't be afraid, my Father, all our prisoners taken at Kentucke are alive and well, we love them, and so do our young women.

Some of your people mend our guns, and others tell us they can make more of the same. These are now the same as we. In one moon after this, we will go with them to their friends at Kentucke. Some of your people will now go

with

Sorry:
The defect on the previous page was that way in the original book we reproduced.

with Coftea, a Chief of our nation, to fee his Great Father, the Long Knife, at the Falls of Ohio.

My Father,

This being the day of joy to the Wabafh Indians, we beg a little drop of your milk, to let our warriors fee it came from your own breaft. We were born and raifed in the woods; we could never learn to make rum—God has made the White Flefh mafters of the world; they make every thing; and we all love rum————

Then they delivered three ftrings of blue and white wampum, and the coronet of peace.

PRESENT, in COUNCIL,

MUSKITO,
Capt. BEAVER,
WOODS & BURNING,
BADTRIPES,
ANTIA,
MONTOUR,
CASTIA,
GRAND COURT;

With many other Chiefs, and War Captains, and the Principal Inhabitants of the Poft of St. Vincent's.

O f

OF THE INDIANS.

WE have an account of twenty-eight different nations of Indians, Eaſtward of the Miſſiſſippi.—Their ſituation is as follows.

The Cherokee Indians are neareſt to Kentucke, living upon the Teneſe River, near the mouths of Clench, Holſtein, Nolachucke, and French-Broad Rivers, which form the Teneſe or Cherokee River, in the interior parts of North-Carolina, two hundred miles from Kentucke.

The Chicamawgees live about ninety miles down the Teneſe from the Cherokees, at a place called Chicamawgee, which in our language ſignifies a Boiling Pot, there being a whirl-pool in the river dangerous for boats. The Dragomonough, a Chief of the Cherokees, with ſixty more, broke off from that nation, and formed this tribe,

tribe, which is called by the name of the Whirl-
pool.

The Cheegees, and Middle Settlement Indians, are settled about fifty and eighty miles South
of the Cherokees. These four tribes speak one
language, being descended from the Cherokees.

The Chicasaws inhabit about one hundred
miles N. W. from our settlement at French
Lick, on Cumberland River, on the heads of a
river called Tombecbe, which runs into Mobile
Bay.

The Cheftaw nation are eighty miles from the
Chicasaws, near the same river.

The Creek Indians live about one hundred and
fifty miles South of the Chicasaws, on the Apa-
lacicola river, which runs into the Gulph of Mexico, some little distance East of Mobile Bay.

The Chaco nation are by four different
names of residences, viz. the Low... Joac's, the
Ticks of St. Marys, and the St. Turruches, and
the head of St. Lucy. These live on the
borders of Georgia, and run separately into the
ocean

The Catauba Indians are settled in North Carolina,

Sorry:

The defect on the previous page was that way in the original book we reproduced.

rolina, about two hundred miles diftant from Charles-town, in S. Carolina.

The tribes to the Weftward of Ohio River are the Delawares, living upon the Mifkingum River, which runs into the Ohio one hundred and eighty-feven miles above Sciotha, on the N. Weft fide.

The Mingo Nation lives upon a N. W. branch of Sciotha River, as is reprefented in the map.

The Wyandotts poffefs the banks of a river called Sandufky, which heads and interlocks with Sciotha, and, running in a contrary direction nearly N. W. for a great diftance, falls into Lake Erie.

The Six Nations are fettled upon waters running into Lake Ontario, that head in the mountain, from whence the Ohio and Sufquehannah rivers rife.

The Shawanefe Indians occupy five towns on the waters of Little and Great Miami, as appears in the map.

The Gibbaways are fixed on the Eaft fide of Detroit River, and oppofite the fort of that name. This river runs out of Lake Huron into

M

into Lake Erie, is thirty-six miles in length, and the fort ftands on the Weft fide, half way betwixt thefe lakes.

The Hurons live fix miles from the Gibbaways, towards Lake Huron, and on the fame fide of the river.

The Tawaws are found eighteen miles up the Mawmee or Omee River, which runs into Lake Erie.

There is a fmall tribe of Tawas fettled at a place called the Rapids, fome diftance higher up the river than the former.

The Mawmee Indians live two hundred and forty miles up this river, at a place called Rofedebeau.

The Piankafhaws refide about one hundred and fixty miles up Wabafh River :—

The Vermilion Indians about fixty miles higher;—and the Wyahtinaws about thirty miles ftill further up the fame river.

The Wabafh heads and interlocks with Mawmee, and runs a contrary direction into Ohio, three hundred and eighteen miles below the Falls.

The

The Long-ifle or Ifle-River Indians live on Ifle, or White River, which runs into Wabafh.

The Kickapoos are fixed on a branch of Mawmee River above the Long-ifle Indians.

The Ozaw Nation lives on the Ozaw River, which runs into Miffiffippi :——

And the Kakafky Nation, on the Miffiffippi, two hundred miles above the Ozaws.

The Illinois Indians inhabit upon the Illinois River, which falls into the Miffiffippi ;——

And the Poutawottamies near St. Jofeph's, a town on a branch of the Illinois.

The Sioux and Renards, are neighbours to the fort of Michillimackinac, on Lake Michigan.

Thefe are the principal part of the Nations within the limits of the United States. Allowing about feven hundred to a nation or tribe, they will contain, in all, twenty thoufand fouls, and confequently may furnifh between four and five thoufand warriors.

The Speculations of curious idlenefs have framed
ed

ed many fyftems to account for the population of this immenfe continent. There is fcarce a people in the old world which has not had its advocates; and there have not been wanting fome, who, defpairing to loofen, have cut the knot, by fuppofing that the power, which furnifhed America with plants, has in the fame manner fupplied it with men, or at leaft, that a remnant in this continent was faved from the univerfal deluge, as well as in the other. As this fubject is rather curious than ufeful, and, in its very nature, does not admit of certainty, every thing that paffed in America before the arrival of the Europeans being plunged in Cimmerian darknefs, except thofe little traditional records, which diffufe a glimmering light on the two empires of Mexico and Peru, for about two hundred years at moft before that period, we fhall only flightly touch on that fubject; chiefly for the fake of taking notice of fome modern difcoveries which feem to ftrengthen the probability of fome former theories. The great fimilarity, or rather identity, of the perfons and manners of the Americans, and thofe of the Tartars of the N. Eaftern parts of Afia, together with a prefumption, which has long poffeffed the learned, that Afia and America were united, or at leaft feparated only by a narrow fea, has inclined the more reflecting part of mankind to the opinion, that the true origin of the Indians is from this quarter. The immenfe feas, which feparate the

two

two continents on every other fide, render it highly improbable that any colonies could ever have
been fent a-crofs them before the difcovery of the
magnetical compafs. The ingenious M. Buffon
too has remarked, and the obfervation appears to
be juft, that there are no animals inhabiting in
common the two continents, but fuch as can bear
the colds of the North. Thus there are no ele-
phants, no lions, no tigers, no camels in America; but bears, wolves, deer, and elks in abundance, abfolutely the fame in both hemifpheres.
This hypothefis, which has been gaining ground
ever fince its firft appearance in the world, is
now reduced almoft to a certainty by the late difcoveries of Capt. Cook. That illuftrious, but
unfortunate navigator, in his laft voyage, pene-
trated for a confiderable diftance into the ftrait
which divides Afia from America, which is only
fix leagues wide at its mouth ; and therefore eafily practicable for canoes. We may now therefore conclude, that no farther enquiry will ever be
made in to the general origin of the American tribes.

Yet, after all, it is far from being improbable that
various nations, by fhipwreck, or otherwife, may
have contributed, in fome degree, to the population of this continent. The Carthaginians, who
had many fettlements on the coaft of Africa, beyond the Straits of Gibraltar, and pufhed their
difcoveries as far as where the two continents in
that

that quarter approach each other the neareft, may probably have been thrown by tempefts on the American coaft, and the companies of the veffels finding it impracticable to return, may have incorporated with the former inhabitants, or have formed new fettlements, which, from want of the neceffary inftruments to exercife the arts they were acquainted with, would naturally degenerate into barbarity. There are indeed fome ancient writers, who give us reafon to fuppofe, that there were colonies regularly formed by that nation in America, and that the communication, after having continued for fome time, was ftopped by order of the State. But it is difficult to conceive that any people, eftablifhed with all thofe neceffaries proper for their fituation, fhould ever degenerate, from fo high a degree of cultivation as the Carthaginians poffeffed, to a total ignorance even of the moft neceffary arts : And therefore it feems probable, that if that nation ever had fuch colonies, they muft have been cut off by the natives, and every veftige of them deftroyed.

About the ninth and tenth centuries, the Danes were the greateft navigators in the univerfe. They difcovered and fettled Iceland ; and from thence, in 964, planted a colony in Greenland. The ancient Icelandic chronicles, as reported by M. Mallet, contain an account of fome Icelanders,
who,

who, in the clofe of an unfuccefsful war, fled to Greenland, and from thence Weftward, to a country covered with vines, which from thence they called Vinland.

The adventurers returned home, and conducted a colony to their new difcovery; but difturbances arifing in Denmark, all communication with Greenland, as well as Vinland, ceafed; and thofe countries remained unknown to the reft of the world for feveral ages. The remains of this colony are probably to be found on the coaft of Labrador, in the nation of the Efquimaux. The colour of their fkins, their hairy bodies and bufhy beards, not to mention the difference of manners, mark an origin totally diftinct from that of the other Indians.

In the year 1170, Madoc, fon of Owen Gwynnedh, Prince of Wales, diffatisfied with the fituation of affairs at home, left his country, as related by the Welfh hiftorians, in queft of new fettlements, and leaving Ireland to the North, proceeded Weft till he difcovered a fertile country; where, leaving a colony, he returned, and perfuading many of his country-men to join him, put to fea with ten fhips, and was never more heard of.

This

This account has, at several times, drawn the attention of the world; but as no vestiges of them had then been found, it was concluded, perhaps too rashly, to be a fable, or at least, that no remains of the colony existed. Of late years, however, the Western settlers have received frequent accounts of a nation, inhabiting at a great distance up the Missouri, in manners and appearance resembling the other Indians, but speaking Welsh, and retaining some ceremonies of the christian worship; and at length, this is universally believed there to be a fact.

Captain Abraham Chaplain, of Kentucke, a gentleman, whose veracity may be entirely depended upon, assured the author, that in the late war, being with his company in garrison at Kaskasky, some Indians came there, and, speaking in the Welsh dialect, were perfectly understood and conversed with by two Welshmen in his company, and that they informed them of the situation of their nation as mentioned above.

The author is sensible of the ridicule which the vain and the petulant may attempt to throw on this account; but as truth only has guided his pen, he is regardless of the consequences, and flatters himself, that, by calling the attention of mankind once more to this subject, he may be the means of procuring a more accurate inquiry

into

into its truth, which, if it fhould even refute
the ftory of the Welfh, will at leaft perform the
important fervice to the world, of promoting a
more accurate difcovery of this immenfe continent.

There are feveral ancient remains in Kentucke,
which feem to prove, that this country was formerly inhabited by a nation farther advanced in
the arts of life than the Indians. Thefe are there
ufually attributed to the Welfh, who are fuppofed to have formerly inhabited here ; but having
been expelled by the natives, were forced to take
refuge near the fources of the Miffouri.

It is well known, that no Indian nation has e-
ver practifed the method of defending themfelves
by entrenchments ; and fuch a work would even
be no eafy one, while thefe nations were unac-
quainted with the ufe of iron.

In the neighbourhood of Lexington, the remains of two ancient fortifications are to be feen,
furnifhed with ditches and baftions. One of
thefe contains about fix acres of land, and the o-
ther nearly three. They are now overgrown with
trees, which, by the number of circles in the
wood, appear to be not lefs than one hundred
and fixty years old. Pieces of earthen veffels
have alfo been plowed up near Lexington, a ma-

N   nufacture

nufacture with which the Indians were never acquainted.

The burying-grounds, which were mentioned above, under the head of Curiofities, form another ftrong argument that this country was formerly inhabited by a people different from the prefent Indians. Although they do not difcover any marks of extraordinary art in the ftructure, yet, as many nations are particularly tenacious of their ancient cuftoms, it may perhaps be worthy of enquiry, whether thefe repofitories of the dead do not bear a confiderable refemblance to the ancient Britifh remains. Some buildings, attributed to the Picts, are mentioned by the Scottifh antiquaries, which, if the author miftakes not, are formed nearly in the fame manner. Let it be enough for him to point out the road, and hazard fome uncertain conjectures. The day is not far diftant, when the fartheft receffes of this continent will be explored, and the accounts of the Welfh eftablifhed beyond the poffibility of a doubt, or configned to that oblivion which has already received fo many fuppofitions founded on arguments as plaufible as thefe.

PERSONS AND HABITS.

THE Indians are not born white; and take
a great

a great deal of pains to darken their complexion, by anointing themfelves with greafe, and lying in the fun. They alfo paint their faces, breafts and fhoulders, of various colours, but generally red; and their features are well formed, efpecially thofe of the women. They are of a middle ftature, their limbs clean and ftraight, and fcarcely any crooked or deformed perfon is to be found among them. In many parts of their bodies they prick in gun-powder in very pretty figures. They fhave, or pluck the hair off their heads, except a patch about the crown, which is ornamented with beautiful feathers, beads, wampum, and fuch like baubles. Their ears are pared, and ftretched in a thong down to their fhoulders. They are wound round with wire to expand them, and adorned with filver pendants, rings, and bells, which they likewife wear in their nofes. Some of them will have a large feather through the cartilage of the nofe; and thofe who can afford it, wear a collar of wampum, a filver breaftplate, and bracelets, on the arms and wrifts. A bit of cloth about the middle, a fhirt of the Englifh make, on which they beftow innumerable broaches to adorn it, a fort of cloth boots and mockafons, which are fhoes of a make peculiar to the Indians, ornamented with porcupine quills, with a blanket or match-coat thrown over all, compleats their drefs at home; but when they go to war, they leave their trinkets behind, and

mere

mere neceſſaries ſerve them. There is little difference between the dreſs of the men and women, excepting that a ſhort petticoat, and the hair, which is exceeding black, and long, clubbed behind, diſtinguiſh ſome of the latter. Except the head and eye-brows, they pluck the hair, with great diligence, from all parts of the body, eſpecially the looſer part of the ſex.

Their warlike arms are guns, bows and arrows, darts, ſcalping-knives and tomahawks. This is one of their moſt uſeful pieces of field-furniture, ſerving all the offices of the hatchet, pipe, and ſword. They are exceeding expert in throwing it, and will kill at a conſiderable diſtance. The world has no better marks-men, with any weapon. They will kill birds flying, fiſhes ſwimming, and wild beaſts running.

G E N I U S.

THE Indians are not ſo ignorant as ſome ſuppoſe them, but are a very underſtanding people, quick of apprehenſion, ſudden in execution, ſubtle in buſineſs, exquiſite in invention, and induſtrious in action. They are of a very gentle and amiable diſpoſition to thoſe they think their friends, but as implacable in their enmity; their revenge being only compleated, in the entire

tire deftruction of their enemies. They are very hardy, bearing heat, cold, hunger and thirft, in a furprifing manner, and yet no people are more addicted to excefs in eating and drinking, when it is conveniently in their power. The follies, nay mifchief, they commit when inebriated, are entirely laid to the liquor, and no one will revenge any injury (murder excepted) received from one who is no more himfelf. Among the Indians, all men are equal, perfonal qualities being moft efteemed. No diftinction of birth, no rank, renders any man capable of doing prejudice to the rights of private perfons; and there is no pre-eminence from merit, which begets pride, and which makes others too fenfible of their own inferiority. Though there is perhaps lefs delicacy of fentiment in the Indians than amongft us ; there is, however, abundantly more probity, with infinitely lefs ceremony, or equivocal compliments. Their public conferences fhew them to be men of genius ; and they have, in a high degree, the talent of natural eloquence.

They live difperfed in fmall villages, either in the woods, or on the banks of rivers, where they have little plantations of Indian-corn, and roots, not enough to fupply their families half the year, and fubfifting the remainder of it by hunting, fifhing and fowling, and the fruits of
the

the earth, which grow fpontaneoufly in great plenty.

Their huts are generally built of fmall logs, and covered with bark, each one having a chimney, and a door, on which they place a padlock.

Old Chelicothe is built in form of a Kentucke ftation, that is, a parallelogram, or long fquare; and fome of their houfes are fhingled A long Council-houfe extends the whole length of the town, where the King and Chiefs of the nation frequently meet, and confult of all matters of importance, whether of a civil or military nature.

Some huts are built by fetting up a frame on forks, and placing bark againft it; others of reeds, and furrounded with clay. The fire is in the middle of the wigwam, and the fmoke paffes through a little hole. They join reeds together by cords run through them, which ferve them for tables and beds. They moftly lie upon fkins of wild beafts, and fit on the ground. They have brafs kettles and pots to boil their food; gourds or calabafhes, cut afunder, ferve them for pails, cups and difhes.

RELIGION.

RELIGION.

THE accounts of travellers, concerning their religion, are various; and although it cannot be abfolutely affirmed that they have none, yet it muft be confeffed very difficult to define what it is. All agree that they acknowledge one Supreme God, but do not adore him. They have not feen him, they do not know him, believing him to be too far exalted above them, and too happy in himfelf to be concerned about the trifling affairs of poor mortals. They feem alfo to believe in a future ftate, and that after death they fhall be removed to their friends who have gone before them, to an elyfium, or paradife.

The Wyandotts, near Detroit, and fome others, have the Roman Catholic religion introduced amongft them by miffionaries. Thefe have a church, a minifter, and a regular burying-ground. Many of them appear zealous, and fay prayers in their families. Thefe, by acquaintance with white people, are a little civilized, which muft of neceffity precede chriftianity.

The Shawanefe, Cherokees, Chickafaws, and fome others, are little concerned about fuperftition, or religion. Others continue their former fuperftitious worfhip of the objects of their love

and

and fear, and efpecially thofe beings whom they moft dread, and whom therefore we generally denominate devils; though, at the fame time, it is allowed they pray to the fun, and other inferior benevolent deities, for fuccefs in their undertakings, for plenty of food, and other neceffaries in life.

They have their feftivals, and other rejoicing-days, on which they fing and dance in a ring, taking hands, having fo painted and difguifed themfelves, that it is difficult to know any of them; and after enjoying this diverfion for a while, they retire to the place where they have prepared a feaft of fifh, flefh, fowls and fruits; to which all are invited, and entertained with their country fongs. They believe that there is great virtue in feafts for the fick. For this purpofe a young buck muft be killed, and boiled, the friends and near neighbours of the patient invited, and having firft thrown tobacco on the the fire, and covered it up clofe, they all fit down in a ring, and raife a lamentable cry. They then uncover the fire, and kindle it up; and the head of the buck is firft fent about, every one taking a bit, and giving a loud croak, in imitation of crows. They afterwards proceed to eat all the buck, making a moft harmonious, melancholy fong; in which ftrain their mufic is particularly excellent.

As

As they approach their towns, when some of their people are lost in war, they make great lamentations for their dead, and bear them long after in remembrance.

Some nations abhor adultery, do not approve of a plurality of wives, and are not guilty of theft; but there are other tribes that are not so scrupulous in these matters. Amongst the Chickasaws a husband may cut off the nose of his wife, if guilty of adultery; but men are allowed greater liberty. This nation despises a thief. Among the Cherokees they cut off the nose and ears of an adulteress; afterwards her husband gives her a discharge; and from this time she is not permitted to refuse any one who presents himself. Fornication is unnoticed; for they allow persons in a single state unbounded freedom.

Their form of marriage is short—the man, before witnesses, gives the bride a deer's foot, and she, in return, presents him with an ear of corn, as emblems of their several duties.

The women are very slaves to the men; which is a common case in rude, unpolished nations, throughout the world. They are charged with being revengeful; but this revenge is only doing themselves justice on those who injure them,

O   and

and is feldom executed, but in cafes of murder and adultery.

Their king has no power to put any one to death by his own authority; but the murderer is generally delivered up to the friends of the deceafed, to do as they pleafe. When one kills another, his friend kills him, and fo they continue until much blood is fhed; and at laft, the quarrel is ended by mutual prefents. Their kings are hereditary, but their authority extremely limited. No people are a more ftriking evidence of the miferies of mankind in the want of government than they. Every chief, when offended, breaks off with a party, fettles at fome diftance, and then commences hoftilities againft his own people. They are generally at war with each other. Thefe are common circumftances amongft the Indians.

When they take captives in war, they are exceedingly cruel, treating the unhappy prifoners in fuch a manner, that death would be preferable to life. They afterwards give them plenty of food, load them with burdens, and when they arrive at their towns, they muft run the gauntlet. In this, the favages exercife fo much cruelty, that one would think it impoffible they fhould furvive their fufferings. Many are killed; but if one outlives this trial, he is adopted into a family as a

fon,

fon, and treated with paternal kindnefs; and if he avoids their fufpicions of going away, is allowed the fame privileges as their own people.

The CONCLUSION.

HAVING finifhed my intended narrative, I fhall clofe the appendix, with a few obfervations upon the happy circumftances, that the inhabitants of Kentucke will probably enjoy, from the poffeffion of a country fo extenfive and fertile.

There are four natural qualities neceffary to promote the happinefs of a country, viz. A good foil, air, water and trade. Thefe taken collectively, excepting the latter, Kentucke poffeffes in a fuperior degree: And, agreeable to our defcription of the weftern trade, we conclude, that it will be nearly equal to any other on the continent of America, and the difadvantages it is fubject to, be fully compenfated by the fertility of the foil.

This fertile region, abounding with all the luxuries of nature, ftored with all the principal materials for art and induftry, inhabited by virtuous and ingenious citizens, muft univerfally attract the attention of mankind, being fituated in the central part of the extenfive American empire,

pire, (the limits of whofe ample domains, as deſcribed in the ſecond article of the late Definitive Treaty, are fubjoined) where agriculture, induſtry, laws, arts and ſciences, flouriſh ; where afflicted humanity raiſes her drooping head ; where ſprings a harveſt for the poor ; where conſcience ceaſes to be a ſlave, and laws are no more than the ſecurity of happineſs ; where nature makes reparation for having created man ; and government, ſo long proſtituted to the moſt criminal purpoſes, eſtabliſhes an afylum in the wilderneſs for the diſtreſſed of mankind.

The recital of your happineſs will call to your country all the unfortunate of the earth, who, having experienced oppreſſion, political or religious, will there find a deliverance from their chains. To you innumerable multitudes will emigrate from the hateful regions of deſpotiſm and tyranny; and you will ſurely welcome them as friends, as brothers; you will welcome them to partake with you of your happineſs.—Let the memory of Lycurgus, the Spartan legiſlator, who baniſhed covetouſneſs, and the love of gold from his country ; the excellent Locke, who firſt taught the doctrine of toleration ; the venerable Penn, the firſt who founded a city of brethren ; and Waſhington, the defender and protector of perſecuted liberty, be ever the illuſtrious examples of your political conduct. Avail yourſelves

of

of the benefits of nature, and of the fruitful country you inhabit.

Let the iron of your mines, the wool of your
flocks, your flax and hemp, the skins of the ſavage animals that wander in your woods, be fa-
ſhioned into manufactures, and take an extraordinary value from your hands. Then will you
rival the ſuperfluities of Europe, and know that
happineſs may be found, without the commerce
ſo univerſally deſired by mankind.

In your country, like the land of promiſe,
flowing with milk and honey, a land of brooks
of water, of fountains and depths, that ſpring
out of valleys and hills, a land of wheat and
barley, and all kinds of fruits, you ſhall eat
bread without ſcarceneſs, and not lack any thing
in it ; where you are neither chilled with the
cold of capricorn, nor ſcorched with the burning heat of cancer ; the mildneſs of your air ſo
great, that you neither feel the effects of infec-
ti us fogs, nor peſtilential vapours. Thus, your
c untry, favoured with the ſmiles of heaven,
will probably be inhabited by the firſt people the
world ever knew.

ARTICLE

ARTICLE II. *of the late* DEFINITIVE TREATY.

A N D that all difputes which might arife in
future on the fubject of the boundaries of the
faid United States, may be prevented, it is here-
by agreed and declared, that the following are
and fhall be their boundaries, viz. From the N. W.
angle of Nova-Scotia, viz. that angle which is
formed by a line drawn due North from the
fource of St. Croix River to the Highlands, along
the faid Highlands, which divide thofe rivers
that empty themfelves into the river St. Lawrence, from thofe which fall into the Atlantic o-
cean, to the North-Wefternmoft head of Con-
necticut River ; thence down along the middle of
that river to the forty-fifth degree of North latitude ; from thence by a line due Weft on faid latitude, until it ftrikes the river Iroquois, or Ca-
taraqui ; thence along the middle of the faid river into Lake Ontario, through the middle of the
faid lake, until it ftrikes the communication by
water between that lake and Lake Erie ; thence
along the middle of faid communication into Lake
Erie, through the middle of faid lake until it ar-
rives at the water communication between that
lake and Lake Huron ; thence along the middle of faid water communication into the Lake
Huron ; thence through the middle of faid
lake to the water communication between
that

that lake and Lake Superior; thence through
Lake Superior Northward of the Isles Roy-
al and Phelipeaux to the Long Lake; thence
through the middle of said Long Lake and the
water communication between it and the Lake of
the Woods, to the Lake of the Woods; thence
through the said lake to the most N.W. point thereof, and from thence on a due West course to the
river Mississippi; thence by a line to be drawn a-
long the middle of the said river Mississippi until it shall intersect the Northernmost part of the
thirty-first degree of North latitude; South, by
a line to be drawn due East from the determination of the last mentioned in the latitude of
thirty-one degrees North of the equator, to the
middle of the river Apalachicola, or Catanouche;
thence along the middle thereof to its junction
with the Flint River; thence straight to the
head of St. Mary's River; and thence down a-
long the middle of St. Mary's River to the Atlantic ocean; East, by a line to be drawn along the
middle of the river St. Croix, from its mouth in the
bay of Fundy to its source, and from its source
directly North to the aforesaid Highlands which
divide the rivers that fall into the Atlantic ocean
from those which fall into the river St. Lawrence,
comprehending all islands within twenty leagues
of any part of the shores of the United States,
and lying between lines to be drawn due East
from the points where the aforesaid boundaries
between

between Nova-Scotia on the one part, and East-Florida on the other, shall respectively touch the bay of Fundy and the Atlantic ocean, excepting such islands as now are, or hertofore have been, within the limits of the said province of Nova-Scotia.

ROADS

ROAD from Philadelpia to the Falls of
the Ohio by land.

	M	M.D
FROM Philadelphia to Lancaster	66	
To Wright's on Sufquehannah	10	76
To York-town	12	88
Abbott's-town	15	103
Hunter's-town	10	113
the mountain at Black's Gap	3	116
the other fide of the mountain	7	123
the Stone-houfe Tavern	25	148
Wadkin's Ferry on Potowmack	14	162
Martinfburg	13	175
Winchefter	20	195
Newtown	8	203
Stover's-town	10	213
Woodftock	12	225
Shanandoah River	15	240
the North branch of Shanandoah	29	269
Stanton	15	284
the North Fork of James River	37	321
James River	18	339
Botetourt Court-houfe	12	351
Woods's on Catauba River	21	372
Patterfon's on Roanoak	9	381
the Allegany Mountain	8	389
New River	12	401
the forks of the road	16	417

P   To

	M	M.D
To Fort Chiffel - -	12	429
a Stone Mill - -	11	440
Boyd's - - -	8	448
head of Holftein - -	5	453
Wafhington Court-houfe -	45	498
the Block-houfe - - -	35	533
Powel's Mountain - -	33	566
Walden's Ridge - - -	3	569
the Valley Station - -	4	573
Martin Cabbin's - -	25	598
Cumberland Mountain -	20	618
the ford ot Cumberland River	13	631
the Flat Lick - -	9	640
Stinking Creek - -	2	642
Richland Creek - -	7	649
Down Richland Creek - -	8	657
Rackoon Spring - -	6	663
Laurel River - -	2	665
Hazle Patch - - -	15	680
the ford on Rock-Caftle River	10	690
Englifh's Station - -	25	715
Col. Edwards's at Crab-Orchard	3	718
Whitley's Station - -	5	723
Logan's Station - -	5	728
Clark's Station - -	7	735
Crow's Station - -	4	739
Harrod's Station - -	3	742
Hariand's - -	4	746
		To

	M	M.D
To Harbifon's – –	10	756
Bard's-town. – –	25	781
the Salt-works – –	25	8c6
. the Falls of the Ohio. –	20	826

Kentucke is fituated about South, 60° Weft from Philadelphia, and, on a ftraight line, may be about fix hundred miles diftant from that city.

ROAD to Pittfburg, and Diftances from thence down the Ohio River to its mouth, and from thence down the Miffiffippi to the Mexican Gulph.

	M	M.D
FROM Philadelphia to Lancafter –	66	
To Middletown – –	26	92
Harris's Ferry –	10	102
Carlifle – –	17	119
Shippenfburgh – –	21	140
Chamber's-town –	11	151
Fort Loudon – –	13	164
Fort Littleton – –	18	182
Juniata Creek – –	19	201

To

	M	M.D
To Bedford – –	14	215
the foot of the Allegany Mountains	15	230
Stony-Creek – – –	15	245
the Eaſt ſide of Laurel Hill	12	257
Fort Ligonier – –	9	266
Pittſburg –	54	320

FROM Pittſburg to Log's-town on the Ohio River, N. ſide,	18	
To Big Beaver-Creek, N. –	11	29
Little Beaver-Creek, N. –	13	42
Yellow-Creek, N. ∟	9	51
Ming's Town – –	18	69
Graſs-Creek, N. – –	2	71
Wheelen-Creek, S. ſide, –	25	96
Grave-Creek, S. –	10	106
the Long-Reach – –	16	122
the end of do. – –	15	137
Miſkingum River, N. –	23	160
Little Kenhawa, S. –	12	172
Hockhocking River, N. –	13	185
Great Kenhawa River, S.	11	196
Great Griandot, S. –	24	220
Big Sandy-Creek, S. –	13	233
Sciotha River, N. –	45	278
Big Buffalo-Lick Creek, S.	24	302
a Large Iſland –	20	322
the Three Iſlands ¬	10	332
Limeſtone-Creek, S. –	7	339
Little Miami, N. –	65	404

To

	M.	M.D.
To Licking River, South fide,	8	412
Great Miami River, N. -	27	439
Big-Bone Creek, S. -	32	471
Kentucke River, S. -	44	515
the Rapids of Ohio -	77	592
Salt River, S. -	23	615
the beginning of the Low Country -	132	747
the firft of the Five Iflands	38	785
Green River, S. -	27	812
a Large Ifland -	58	870
Wabafh River, N. -	40	910
the Great Cave, N. -	62	972
Cumberland River, S. -	33	1005
Tenefe River, S. -	12	1017
Fort Meffia-River, S. -	11	1028
the mouth of Ohio River	46	1074
the Iron Banks, S. -	15	1089
Chickafaw River -	67	1156
the River Margot -	104	1160
St. Francis's River -	70	1230
Akanfa River -	108	1338
Yazaw River -	165	1503
the Grand Gulph -	39	1542
the Little Gulph -	14	1556
Fort Rofalie, at the Natches,	31	1587
the River Rouge -	36	1643
the uppermoft mouth of the Miffiffippi	3	1646

To

	M.	M.D.
To Point Coupée	50	1696
Ibberville	35	1731
the Villages of the Alibama Indians	39	1770
New Orleans, S. fide,	60	1830
the mouths of the Miffiffippi	105	1935

A ftraight line drawn from Pittfburg to the mouth of the Miffiffippi may be computed at two thirds of the diftance by the meanders of the rivers, which will be twelve hundred and ninety miles.

CPSIA information can be obtained
at www.ICGtesting.com
Printed in the USA
BVHW041018090819

555506BV00017B/1351/P